ALASKA'S SEWARD PENINSULA

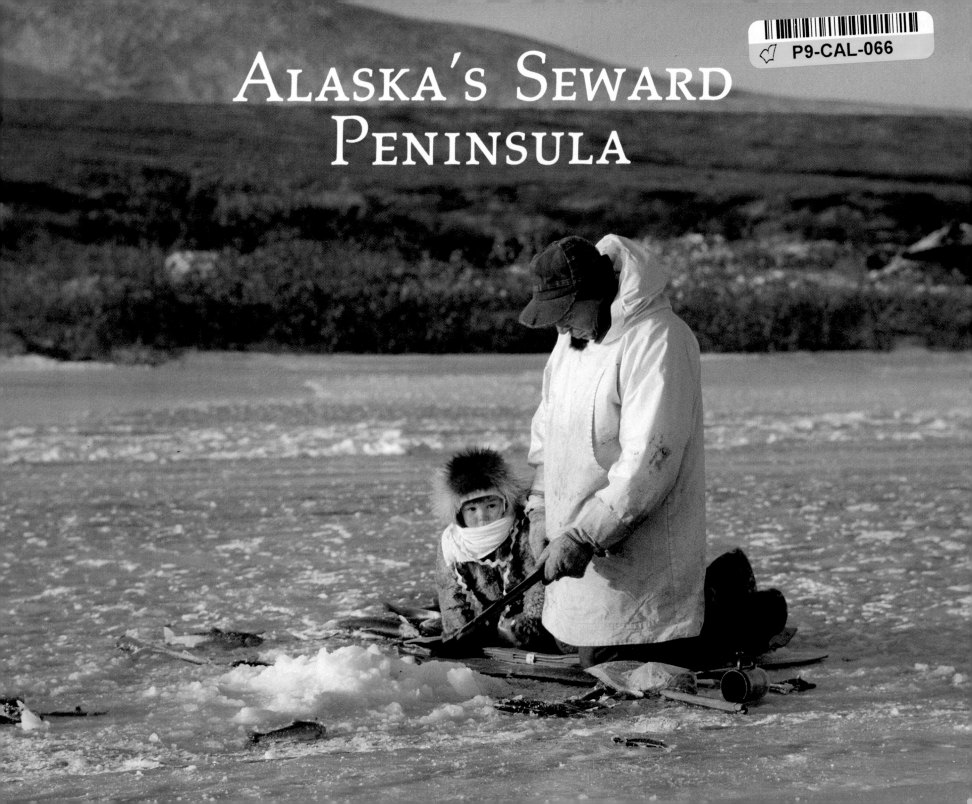

The Alaska Geographic Society

To teach many more to better know and use our natural resources

Editor: Penny Rennick
Associate Editor: Kathy Doogan
Editorial Assistant: Laurie Thompson
Designer: Pamela S. Ernst

ALASKA GEOGRAPHIC®, ISSN 0361-1353, is published quarterly by The Alaska Geographic Society, Anchorage, Alaska 99509-3370. Second-class postage paid in Edmonds, Washington 98020-3588. Printed in U.S.A. Copyright© 1987 by The Alaska Geographic Society. All rights reserved. Registered trademark; Alaska Geographic, ISSN 0361-1353; Key title Alaska Geographic.

THE ALASKA GEOGRAPHIC SOCIETY is a nonprofit organization exploring new frontiers of knowledge across the lands of the polar rim, learning how other men and other countries live in their Norths, putting the geography book back in the classroom, exploring new methods of teaching and learning — sharing in the excitement of discovery in man's wonderful new world north of 51°16'.

MEMBERS OF THE SOCIETY RECEIVE *Alaska Geographic®*, a quality magazine which devotes each quarterly issue to monographic in-depth coverage of a northern geographic region or resource-oriented subject.

The cover — A lone ice fisherman tries his luck offshore from Brevig Mission, a tiny settlement of about 150 on the north shore of Port Clarence. (Roz Goodman)

This tripod, which stands at a point between Koyuk and Dime Landing, marks an old dog team mail trail from Norton Sound across the Seward Peninsula to Candle. (Don Gillespie) **Preceeding page —** An angler and his young helper try their luck fishing through the ice near Nome. (Kory Matthews)

MEMBERSHIP DUES in The Alaska Geographic Society are $30 per year; $34 to non-U.S. addresses. (Eighty percent of each year's dues is for a one-year subscription to *Alaska Geographic®*.) Order from The Alaska Geographic Society, Box 93370, Anchorage, Alaska 99509-3370; (907) 258-2515.

MATERIAL SOUGHT: The editors of *Alaska Geographic®* seek a wide variety of informative material on the lands north of 51°16' on geographic subjects —, anything to do with resources and their uses (with heavy emphasis on quality color photography) — from Alaska, northern Canada, Siberia, Japan — all geographic areas that have a relationship to Alaska in a physical or economic sense. We do not want material done in excessive scientific terminology. We welcome photo submissions (please write for list of upcoming topics), however, we cannot be responsible for submissions not accompanied by sufficient postage for return by certified mail. Payments are made for all material upon publication.

CHANGE OF ADDRESS: The post office does not automatically forward *Alaska Geographic®* when you move. To ensure continous service, notify us six weeks before moving. Send us your new address and zip code (and moving date), your old address and zip code, and if possible send a mailing label from a copy of *Alaska Geographic®*. Send this information to *Alaska Geographic®* Mailing Offices, 130 Second Avenue South, Edmonds, Washington 98020-3588.

MAILING LISTS: We have begun making our members' names and addresses available to carefully screened publications and companies whose products and activities might be of interest to you. If you would prefer not to receive such mailings, please so advise us, and include your mailing label (or your name and address if label is not available).

ABOUT THIS ISSUE: We have called upon some old-timers and contemporary explorers to put together this issue on Alaska's prehistoric gateway, the Seward Peninsula. Robert Steiner, born on the peninsula seven decades ago, tells about growing up in an isolated gold mining town. Robert's father, Otto, came north with the Klondike rush and stayed. His son has shared Otto's notes, giving readers a first-hand account of roaming the Seward Peninsula in search of gold. Bill Sheppard has prepared an overview of the reindeer industry, for decades a major factor in the economy and subsistence lifestyle of Seward Peninsula. Teacher Charlie Crangle opens the door to St. Lawrence Island, homeland of the Siberian Yupik. And biologist and writer Elaine Rhode shares her knowledge of the Bering Sea wilderness of St. Matthew and Hall islands. Penny Rennick, editor of the *Alaska Geographic®* series, contributes the remainder of the text, hoping to share with readers the feeling of timelessness and welcome that radiates from her most favorite corner of Alaska.

We thank the many fine photographers whose images capture the land and people of the Seward Peninsula. We are grateful to Rolfe Buzzell for sharing his knowledge of the Solomon area, and to biologist Bob Nelson for reviewing portions of the manuscript.

The Library of Congress has cataloged this serial publication as follows:

Alaska Geographic. v.1-
    [Anchorage, Alaska Geographic Society] 1972-
    v. ill. (part col.). 23 x 31 cm.
    Quarterly.
    Official publication of the Alaska Geographic Society.
    Key title: Alaska geographic, ISSN 0361-1353.

    1. Alaska — Description and travel — 1959-
    —Periodicals.   I. Alaska Geographic Society.

F901.A266   917.98'04'505   72-92087
                                                         MARC-S
Library of Congress   75[7912]

Table of Contents

The Bering Strait area is still commonly visualized as a narrow path or trail over which people hustled, in one direction, on their way to take up positions in which they would presently be discovered . . . . In fact, the Bering Land Bridge was an enormous continental area extending nearly 1,500 km [900 miles] from its southern extremity, now the eastern Aleutians, to its northern margin in the Arctic Ocean. It was an area that could accommodate many permanent residents, human and animal, and it endured for a longer time than that documented for the entire period of human occupancy in America.

. . . William S. Laughlin
VII Congress of the International
Association for Quaternary
Research and
The Bering Land Bridge (1967)

On the Edge of Tomorrow

Sitting on the razorback above the village of Wales, I could easily see why a wanderer from San Francisco thought he could walk to Siberia, or why a French baron windsurfed across Bering Strait to the Soviet Union. After all, mysterious and forbidden Siberia is right there, enticing. Only 25 miles separate Cape Prince of Wales from Little Diomede Island, and from there it's a mere three miles across the International Dateline and an international boundary to Big Diomede, outpost of a massive continent. Another 28 miles or so and anyone can set foot on Siberia.

On a clear day, East Cape and much more of the Siberian coastline is visible from the exposed rock on which I perched. To my left, the razorback ran up a little higher to join with Cape Mountain (2,289 feet). Cape Prince of Wales, where the granite talus of the mountain's flanks touches Bering Strait, is the end of the line as far as the continent goes, the westernmost point in mainland North America.

Below, the 150 or so Eskimos of the village of Wales went about their daily business. Some strolled the road to where a bridge spanned a small river. Here, on relatively warm days before the washeteria was built, they bathed. Others continued their walk to the reindeer corrals which circled flat lands near a lagoon. It was the end of June and a helicopter would soon herd reindeer from Clarence Ongtowasruk's herd into the corral for the summer antler harvest.

Next to Andrew Seetook's home, I could see Mrs. Seetook splitting a walrus hide which she would soon put away in the family's underground storage. On a rack out by the airstrip, a polar bear hide dried in the wind. Some children played in the one village street, others gathered at the store. More energetic youngsters roamed the marsh behind the village, while women picked greens on the hillside. Some men were out in skin boats, hunting for marine mammals in the Chukchi Sea. Others visited with Diomeders who had boated over from their island. Some years Diomeders stop at Wales on their way to Kotzebue for the big Fourth of July celebration.

The plane from Nome had just arrived, bringing villagers home and a Columbian from South America who

Icebergs crowd the area south of Bering Strait, providing hauling out areas for walrus and seals.
(Kevin Schafer)

5

Above — Lone Fairway Rock rises from the Bering Sea, 10 miles south of Little Diomede Island. The rock shows the way to a good channel on the east side of Bering Strait, thus its name "Fairway."
(Alissa Crandall)
Clockwise from left — Chuck Lewis and Wayne Henry of Golovin skip their boat across the ice of Golovnin Bay to go herring fishing. From there, they boat down to Unalakleet to fish.
(James Magdanz)
Polar bear skins hang to dry on racks at Wales.
(Roz Goodman)
A Wales villager bulldogs a reindeer from Clarence Ongtowasruk's herd during the annual antler harvest.
(Penny Rennick)
Walter Weyapuk Jr. and another Eskimo from Wales wash the sand from a piece of beluga muktuk. Toby Anungazuk Jr. killed the beluga while out in his boat hunting.
(Penny Rennick)

thought he could get to Diomede from Wales, but he wasn't certain how. Walter Weyapuk Jr., village postmaster, had gathered the mail in his cart and was headed back to the tiny post office, complete with wrought iron railing reminiscent of post offices throughout the country decades ago. (The post office has since been moved to a domed structure, jumping from early 20th century to late in one short move.)

This was a time of plenty for the villagers of Wales. While out in his boat hunting, Toby Anungazuk Jr. killed a mother beluga with a near full-term fetus. It took Toby and several helpers less than 30 minutes to completely butcher the whale, wasting nothing.

A few days later a lone female walrus swam offshore heading north into the Chukchi Sea. Village men climbed to the roofs of their houses lining the shore to fire at the walrus. Finally the mammal, wounded and exhausted, was lured ashore just north of the community by villagers kneeling and barking. Perhaps the walrus thought she was coming ashore where others of her kind were resting, but she was swiftly killed as soon as she hit the sands. This time the men required 45 minutes to butcher the animal, and again nothing was wasted.

On another day, when storm clouds were gathering over Siberia, hundreds of smelt were caught in the surf and tossed ashore along the same sandy beach. Villagers grabbed plastic sacks and scurried along the shore, stuffing the slippery fish in the sacks. Many would be frozen for winter use, but Wales residents looked forward to fresh fish dipped in seal oil.

In a bucket on Walter and Flo Weyapuk's porch, the body of a young seal was soaking in sea water before being cooked. Dinner with the generous Weyapuk family was often a mixture of fish, chicken, wild birds, greens dipped in seal oil, white bread and canned peaches. The muktuk (outer layer of skin and blubber) from Toby's beluga provided a special treat.

The village store supplies some of the items for the Eskimos' daily fare. Supplies in bulk come in by plane, either the mail plane or a charter. If Wales residents don't want to wait for a plane, they can hop in their skiff, round the cape and stop in at Lee's well-stocked store at Tin City.

Once the helicopter came, the pilot began rounding up the reindeer from surrounding hills. As the herd gathered near the lagoon northeast of the village, the villagers headed for the corrals. Adult reindeer were forced into a chute, and when they emerged at the other end, sturdy Eskimos waited to wrestle them to the ground. Other workers quickly clipped the antlers and wrapped rubber bands around the stubs to curb the flow of blood. A few of the larger bulls were castrated so their size would increase during the fall, priming them for butchering for the winter meat supply. A Korean firm purchased the antlers which would be sliced or ground up and eventually sold in the Orient as health aids.

The Eskimos worked and played hard in the 24-hour summer daylight. Late in the evening, they gathered for snertz, a fast-moving, loud version of solitaire, or met in the village street for Eskimo ball. This rousing game is somewhat like free-for-all baseball with only two bases. When the best batters hit, everyone on that team runs for a distant line, hoping to cross it before the opposition touches one of them with the ball.

New and old blend well here in Wales. In some ways the villagers have little, in other ways they share the traditions of a millennium.

... Penny Rennick

Prehistoric Gateway

The Seward Peninsula isn't much to look at really. There are no spectacular mountains, no sheer coastline indented with stark fiords. The region lacks the towering forests of southeastern Alaska. No, the Seward Peninsula isn't flamboyant, just solid and steady. So steady, in fact, that it forms the backbone of the Bering Land Bridge which off and on has linked Asia with North America.

About 200 miles from east to west and 120 miles from north to south, the Seward Peninsula stretches toward Siberia from the western Alaska mainland. The area's northernmost point, Cape Espenberg, lies just beyond the Arctic Circle. Everything west of a line drawn from Unalakleet on the south to the Baldwin Peninsula on the north makes up the Inupiat and Yupik world of the Seward Peninsula. This world extends offshore into the Bering Sea where the Siberian Yupik people make their home on St. Lawrence Island, and where wilderness and wildlife take over on uninhabited St. Matthew and Hall islands, King and Sledge islands, and tiny Fairway Rock.

The land itself results from a mixture of plate tectonics, volcanism and erosion. Movement of crustal plates floating above the earth's mantle carried the raw land to the area now known as the Seward Peninsula. Scientists speculate that perhaps a piece of the plate covering Canada's High Arctic swung west to become northern Alaska. Perhaps the plate came from somewhere else. Much about plate tectonics is conjecture, but the general theory holds.

After the land was in place, volcanism took over, sculpting the terrain with each convulsion or outburst. The peninsula's interior, in particular, was influenced by the fiery turmoil. Beginning 65 million years ago, lava flowed from cracks in the earth, leaving sheets of smooth basalt on the surface. For eons intermittent volcanic activity poured lava onto the landscape, not stopping until 1,000 years ago with the Lost Jim lava flow. Weathering of lava from the various flows documents the geological history of the region, giving scientists an unusual opportunity to study weathering and plant succession in a harsh climate at extreme northern latitudes.

Near Devil Mountain, inland from Cape Espenberg, a different chapter of volcanic history unfolds. Here volcanic

Moist lowlands, abundant lakes and rolling hills characterize much of the Seward Peninsula, a 200-mile arm of western Alaska. Here, wind ruffles the waters of Kuzitrin Lake, near the center of the peninsula and headwaters for the Kuzitrin River. (National Park Service; Bering Land Bridge National Preserve)

boils erupted, spewing steam, ash and small quantities of lava. The results centuries later are wide, shallow maar craters which have now filled with water. White Fish Lake, Devil Mountain Lakes and Killeak Lakes testify to this volcanic spasm.

Permafrost underlies the entire peninsula, manifested on the surface by thaw lakes, pingos, ice wedge polygons and solifluction lobes. These thick sheets develop where the upper layer of soil, unable to drain properly through the permafrost, becomes waterlogged and slips down the slope.

A quick view of the peninsula's landscape shows coastal uplands topped by small mountains in the southern half and extensive lowlands in the north. Mount Osborn, 4,720 feet, in the Kigluaik Mountains, known locally as the Sawtooths, crowns the peninsula's four mountain groups. Though not high by Alaska standards, the York, Kigluaik, Bendeleben and Darby mountains consist of tough rocks that withstood erosion before the Pleistocene glacial epoch and gained additional height as the land bounced back when freed of the weight of ice age glaciers.

In the north, the lowlands sweep to the Chukchi Sea where they are fringed by a system of sandy barrier islands. From Cape Espenberg east, the coastline curves around Kotzebue Sound, past Cape Deceit, site of the earliest records of some North American animals, and on to the Buckland River valley. West beyond Espenberg, the barrier islands begin and run in an unbroken string to Cape Prince of Wales. Shallow lagoons lie just inshore, and the entire coastal lowland is sprinkled with numerous lakes and ponds. A few miles inland from Deering, fresh-water Imuruk Lake, largest on the peninsula, spreads its 28 square miles.

The peninsula's southern coast is a series of uplands and valleys with a narrow coastal strip stretching around Norton Sound to Unalakleet. Port Clarence and Golovnin Bay provide good anchorage on the otherwise exposed coast.

Offshore, the Bering-Chukchi platform offers a smooth table 100 to 500 feet deep from which rise the islands of the Bering: The Diomedes, King, Sledge, Fairway Rock and the Punuk group near St. Lawrence. Largest of the Bering Sea islands, St. Lawrence is a volcanic bedrock plain topped by a few weathered mountains. Isolated St. Matthew and Hall islands are even more rugged with an undulating terrain alternating between steep uplands dropping sharply to the sea and shallow lowlands leaning imperceptibly to touch the Bering.

Several rivers drain the peninsula, providing a route for fish to reach spawning grounds and for men to reach interior settlements. Whenever possible, early settlers chose to travel by river rather than tackle the bumpy, spongy surface of tussocky tundra. The Buckland drains the region's northeastern corner. In the south, several rivers empty into Norton Sound including the Kuzitrin, Niukluk with its chief tributary, the Fish, Koyuk, Ungalik and Shaktoolik. The Snake and Nome rivers gained notoriety when prospectors found color in their gravels, launching the famous rush to Nome. The Snake flows out of the hills behind Nome and dumps its load into Norton Sound at the community's port. A few miles to the east the larger Nome River reaches the sea.

The Unalakleet River curves behind the community of Unalakleet before heading into the Nulato Hills for about 105 miles. Designated a wild and scenic river by the federal government, the river offers a good opportunity for rafters or kayakers seeking to explore the country at the eastern end of Norton Sound.

In the Bendeleben Mountains survive a few permanent ice fields, remnants of glaciers which coated the mountains during the Pleistocene. Many of the lowlands remained ice free, and the interplay between these areas and the glaciated heights provides the key to the ancient peninsula's history as the center span for the Bering Land Bridge by which early man entered the Americas.

During the Pleistocene, when immense ice sheets

covered much of the polar world, the ice absorbed water from the oceans, causing sea level to fall. When the ice retreated, sea level rose. Thus, as the glaciers expanded, more land was exposed by the lowered shoreline. In northwestern North America and eastern Asia, this sequence of events opened a tremendous area, known as Beringia or the Bering Land Bridge, estimated at times to have been 900 miles from north to south. The bridge came and went, its margins expanding, contracting or disappearing altogether in tune with changes in the glaciers. Some scientists maintain that the overland corridor may have been exposed for up to 5,000 years at a time, giving wandering herds of mammals and tribes of humans plenty of opportunity to move back and forth between the continents. Most likely the earliest human migrants did not realize they had populated a new continent. They simply moved to and fro, following the game to secure their own survival.

Geothermal hot springs bubble from several sites on the peninsula. Undoubtedly the most famous are at Serpentine within Bering Land Bridge National Preserve and at Pilgrim in the Pilgrim River valley north of Nome beyond the Kigluaik Mountains. Pilgrim has a long history of human use. The springs were a rest area for miners of the Kougarok district just after the turn of the century. The Catholic Church ran a boarding school nearby, their gardens, greenhouses and buildings warmed by the geothermal bounty. Today, a handful of residents still live in the area, their gardens thriving in the warm earth. Pilots from Nome and elsewhere on the peninsula think nothing of loading their plane and heading for a few hours of relaxing bathing. In 1985 a spur was built off the Nome-Taylor Road for local motorists to reach the hot springs.

Government officials did consider generating electricity for Nome from the geothermal energy at Pilgrim, but measurements indicate the water temperature is just below boiling, cool by geothermal standards. Temperatures at this level are enough to heat greenhouses and nearby homes, but not sufficient to generate power for a community.

Laundry hangs to dry at minus 30 degrees in this photo of Unalakleet taken in 1950. Located at the terminus of the Kaltag Portage, an important trail overland from the Yukon River to the east end of Norton Sound, Unalakleet was the site of an ancient village. In the 1830s, the Russians built a small trading post here. Near the turn of the century, a mission was established at Unalakleet, and the town has since grown into one of the largest in the region.
(Adolph Roseneau, courtesy of David Roseneau)

The waters of Serpentine Hot Springs have long been sought for their healthful properties. Eskimo shamans gathered here in earlier times. When the influence of the shamans had passed, native healers still relied on these waters to help their followers. Today villagers from Shishmaref and Deering, as well as outsiders, still come to Serpentine for a refreshing dip in the springs.
(Terry Doyle)

Eskimos have sought the healing waters of more remote Serpentine for centuries. Winter trails from Shishmaref and other traditional village sites lead to Hot Springs Creek near the northern edge of the peninsula's interior plateau. A tractor trail, traversed by snow machine and dog sled in winter, reaches the springs from the end of the Nome-Taylor (Kougarok) Road. Likely the most visited area of Bering Land Bridge National Preserve, Serpentine not only offers a break from the rigors of a harsh climate, but nearby granite tors, dramatic in a landscape that lacks eye-catching spectacles, lure hikers to explore these Cretaceous-age outcrops.

Seward Peninsula's climate reflects a combination of maritime and continental factors. When the Bering and Chukchi seas are ice free, usually from late June or July until November, ocean waters moderate temperatures, humidity increases and clouds fringe the coastline. Once the sea freezes over, however, more extreme continental influences take hold with lowered temperatures and clearing skies. At Nome, on the coast, January temperatures average from minus 3 degrees F. to plus 12 degrees F. In July the average increases to from 20 degrees F. to 33 degrees F. Eastern and interior portions of the peninsula typically endure more temperature fluctuations and have fewer cloudy days, even in summer. At Unalakleet, summer temperatures range between 42 degrees F. and 61 degrees F., while winter readings generally are minus 5 degrees F. to 12 degrees F.

Measured by season, summer has the most precipitation with more than one-third of the yearly total of 10 inches. Winter snowfall reaches 60 inches annually, and can create substantial drifts when whipped about by the wind. The peninsula's wildlife makes the most of the shifting snow, foraging in areas where wind has cleared the snow and exposed the vegetation.

Wind chill becomes an important factor in surviving the peninsula's winter environment, in extreme cases severely curbing wintertime activities. At Wales and Shishmaref on the western coast, for instance, the chill factor can reach minus 100 degrees F., causing instant freezing of exposed flesh.

Seward Peninsula's varied topography supports an equally varied array of vegetation. Study of the region's plant communities focuses on Bering Land Bridge National Preserve, in the peninsula's center and northwestern quarter, where scientists have an opportunity to observe development of a modern vegetation spectrum and compare it with one from prehistory.

At the recent lava flows around Imuruk Lake, botanists explore the initial colonization of new land by lichens and mosses.

Tundra carpets those parts of the peninsula having well-developed soils. In the lowlands where water saturates the earth and lakes and ponds abound, wet tundra, characterized by mat-forming grasses and sedges, pre-

Above — Goose Creek enters the Noxapaga River at this rich grassland in Bering Land Bridge National Preseve. The preserve takes up about one-third of the peninsula, offering within its boundaries an outdoor laboratory where scientists can study the effects of time and climate on a northern environment.
(National Park Service; Bering Land Bridge National Preserve)

dominates. Midway up the hillsides between the coastal wetlands and drier mountainous areas, moist tundra takes hold. The bane of hikers, the grasses of moist tundra form tiny hillocks, called tussocks, which create uneven footing and send hikers sprawling. For those determined to confine their path to the soggy, lichen and moss-covered channels between the tussocks, the going is slow and the channels are likely to catch their boots and send them careening into the grass.

Higher still, low-growing alpine tundra covers the well-drained ridges and mountain slopes. Here plants grow low to the ground while the same species may grow tall and branch out more in more protected areas farther down the slope.

Sand-loving grasses flourish on the dunes along the peninsula's northwestern shore. Other varieties that have adapted to daily inundation by salt water thrive in the

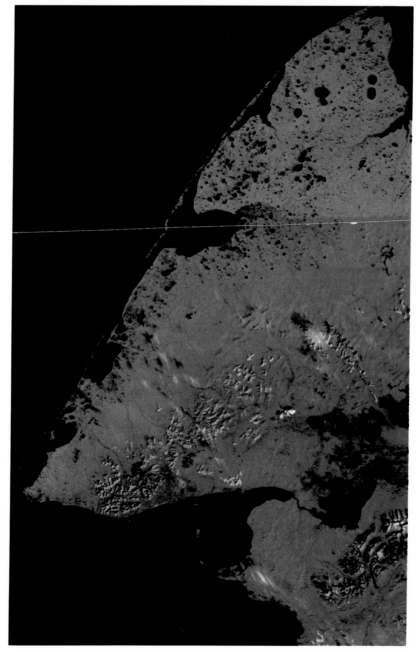

Right — This infrared aerial photo shows the outline of the western peninsula with Cape Prince of Wales on the far left. The dark bodies of water in the lower half are Port Clarence pointing to Imuruk Basin. Where the white line crosses the photo is Shishmaref Inlet, while the community itself lies on the barrier island of Sarichef. The nearly round lakes toward the top of the photo are the maar lakes of White Fish, Devil Mountain and Killeak.
(Courtesy of Don Grybeck)

Above — Abandoned and rusting mining equipment at Bluff tells a story typical of most communities on Seward Peninsula. The town, 21 miles east of Solomon on the shores of Norton Sound, got its start during the gold rush to Nome when miners found color in the beach placers in 1899. Mining ceased in 1956, and today murres and kittiwakes have taken over the cliffs for their nesting colony. (Dee McKenna) **Right** — Residents of Shaktoolik have moved their village site twice in the past 50 years. Now the community of 186 residents is located on high ground between a marshy lowland and the shores of Norton Sound, about 33 miles north of Unalakleet. (Alissa Crandall)

tidal marshes near some river mouths. Brant and emperor geese congregate here also to feed on the estuarine vegetation.

Between the tundra and woodlands grow mixed thickets of willow, alder and birch, excellent browse for the region's moose.

The white spruce forest of Alaska's Interior extends onto the eastern peninsula but reaches its limit in the upper Kugruk and Koyuk river valleys. The interplay between forest and tundra offers scientists one more opportunity to observe how one plant community overcomes another. These observations, in turn, enable them to interpret more precisely the fossil record which indicates that temperate forests covered all of the peninsula in warmer times.

The peninsula's combination of coastal marine environment, tundra and woodlands provides suitable habitat for an abundance of wildlife. In the past 30 years or so moose have expanded their range into northwestern Alaska, including the Seward Peninsula. These huge members of the deer family winter in river valleys where they find their favorite browse, willows. Their numbers have increased to the point that local subsistence hunters, who once focused their efforts entirely on marine mammals, now on occasion turn to moose for their winter meat supply.

While black bears are few and scattered in the more wooded sections of the peninsula, the river valleys in the open country to the west offer abundant food for grizzlies. In spring after the bears leave their dens, they seek carrion, moose and reindeer calves, and berries that survived the winter. Later, they feed on coastal grasses, waiting for salmon to begin their runs upstream to spawning grounds. In fall, the bears once again turn to berries to fatten themselves for winter.

Polar bears come to the northern peninsula with the pack ice in the fall, and Natives hunt them when they can. Older residents such as the elders of Shishmaref like

Above left — The tiny community of Golovin lines the shores of a spit between Golovnin Lagoon and Golovnin Bay 90 miles east of Nome on Norton Sound. (James Magdanz) **Lower left** — Each spring villagers from Brevig Mission head for spring hunting camps along the shores of Brevig Lagoon. (James Magdanz) **Above** — Located on a small spit between Port Clarence and Grantley Harbor, Teller is the terminus of the Nome-Teller Road. The community's approximately 250 residents look to subsistence to sustain their economy. Each year some residents head up the Kuzitrin River to Mary's Igloo and other traditional fishing and hunting sites. (Barbara Winkley)

Above — Transplants of musk oxen in 1970 and 1981 by Alaska Department of Fish and Game biologists form the basis for a herd of about 300 which now roams Seward Peninsula. (Bob Nelson)

Above right — Monarch of northern waters, the omnivorous polar bear feeds on seals or whatever else happens to cross its path. The white bears come south with the pack ice in the fall and are taken by native hunters whenever possible. (Bob Nelson) **Right top** — David Roseneau works his way through grass tussocks for a close look at a flock of murres on Hall Island. (Philip D. Martin)

Right, lower left — Biologist Bill Tilton prepares to release a gyrfalcon in the interior of the Seward Peninsula. (Terry Doyle)

Right, lower right — An arctic fox, its coat changing with the seasons, streaks across the tundra of the Punuk Islands near St. Lawrence Island. (Kevin Schafer)

to eat the meat, but younger Natives go more for the hides, which provide raw materials for arts and crafts.

A portion of the Western Arctic caribou herd winters in some river drainages of the eastern peninsula. In the 1890s, Sheldon Jackson embarked upon his plan to import reindeer from Siberia. Allowed to run wild, reindeer will join with caribou herds. Thus herders made a special attempt to separate the two species.

The region's wolf population is limited, and the animals are confined primarily to wooded areas in the eastern peninsula where there is better cover and some caribou on which to prey.

Shaggy musk oxen also once inhabited most of Seward Peninsula. But they were hunted out, and not until 1970 did the *oomingmak*, or bearded one, again thunder across the tundra. That year biologists from the Alaska Department of Fish and Game transplanted 35 musk oxen to the peninsula. In 1981 they brought in 34 more. Now the peninsula has about 300 musk oxen spread between several main herds and splinter groups.

Small furbearers keep trappers busy throughout the region. Substantial numbers of wolverine occur in every major drainage, and there are plenty of red and cross fox. At times arctic fox are abundant in northern and western areas of the peninsula. Trappers take marten and a few mink in timbered areas in the east where lynx also concentrate. Their chief prey, snowshow hare, nibble the willows in the river valleys, while larger tundra or arctic hare, weighing up to 15 pounds, stick to high country where wind blows the snow cover from their favorite foods. Tundra hare travel in large groups, sometimes up to 50, and bounding away on their hind legs they leave a never-to-be-forgotten vision of a vibrant arctic winter.

Beaver are steadily expanding their territory west, and have reached the Pilgrim River where a family has built a big lodge by the bridge on the Nome-Taylor Road. Muskrat used to be plentiful in the region, but in the past six years or so have become scarce. Arctic ground squirrels scurry throughout most of the peninsula, and are still a favored prey for older Eskimo women who trap them and use the skins to line parkas.

Among the game birds, willow and rock ptarmigan

inhabit the entire peninsula, while sharp-tailed and spruce grouse occur in forested areas.

But game bird species hardly tell the story of the abundant bird life of the Seward Peninsula, whose strategic location near Asia lures exotic species to nest on its tundra-covered hills. An elegant plover, the Eurasian dotterel, comes to the peninsula each summer. The wheatear sings from shrub thickets, while wagtails nest in holes in the tundra, and Lapland longspurs suspend their tiny cupped nests from stalks in the tundra.

Shorebirds and waterfowl make the most of wetlands in the peninsula's northern reaches, just as raptors do the rocky outcrops in the mountains. Endangered arctic peregrine falcons have been recorded here where they plummet from on high to capture other birds on the wing. Bering Sea islands are known for their seabird colonies, but even such mainland headlands as Cape Deceit and Sullivan Bluffs shelter seabirds.

River and marine resources have always been important to the subsistence lifestyle which prevails on the peninsula. A difference in focus separates the region's Natives. Marine mammals play a more important role for those living at the Bering Strait end. Eastward, salmon runs and river resources dominate the annual search for food. Hunters from Gambell, Savoonga and Wales go after the bowhead whale, and Diomeders hope to join them. Buckland and Deering residents, as well as Eskimos from Kotzebue, hunt beluga at a natural trap near Elephant Point on Kotzebue Sound. The St. Lawrence Island subsistence economy depends on walrus meat for food, skins for boats, and ivory for art work. Subsistence hunters throughout the region take seals whenever possible.

Rivers in the eastern area carry large runs of chum and pink salmon, and those near Unalakleet also offer silvers and kings, all of which support a commercial fishery as well as subsistence. An early spring run of herring into the Buckland River offers fishermen a unique opportunity to dry their fish without the insects and higher tempera-

tures which affect runs later in the season. Other species available to peninsula fishermen include grayling, smelt, burbot, arctic char, northern pike and whitefish. Farther west Teller and Brevig Mission residents take salmon from Grantley Harbor, while residents of Nome head north to the Pilgrim River and Salmon Lake, both on the Nome-Taylor Road.

Winter brings the ice fishermen out onto Norton Sound where they jig for tomcod and cut holes big enough to lower pots for red king crab.

The Seward Peninsula provides well for its people, an important factor in a region where the price of groceries can be prohibitive and selections are limited at best.

Facing page, clockwise —
A gray whale surfaces near King Island during its annual migration to summer feeding grounds in polar seas. (Stephen Leatherwood)
Tiny threads protect the inner core of the woolly lousewort from severe winds which can dry the plant. (Kevin Schafer)
Salmon hang out to dry near a newly covered skin boat at Nome. The bright white of the boat helps to camouflage it when the hunters are out among the ice floes searching for marine mammals. (Bob Nelson)
Florence Willoya picks salmonberries on tundra-covered slopes near Golovin. (James Magdanz)
Biologist Lloyd Lowry takes a blood sample from a ribbon seal on an ice floe in the Bering Sea. (Kevin Schafer)
A pod of beluga whales makes its way through a lead in the pack ice near Bering Strait. (Stephen Leatherwood)

19

CANDLE, APRIL 9, 1907.

Ancient Men, Missionaries and Miners

The Seward Peninsula is a modern-day remnant of Beringia, the Bering Land Bridge which off and on linked North America with Asia. Most scientists agree that across this bridge came the prehistoric people who populated the Americas.

Early man arrived in northwestern Alaska perhaps 8,000 to 10,000 years ago (some claim much earlier) when wanderers from northern Asia crossed the land bridge seeking caribou and other land mammals. We call these people members of the American Paleo-Arctic tradition. More than 3,000 years later, individuals of the woodland-oriented Northern Archaic culture migrated to northwest Alaska from the south and east.

Another couple of thousand years passed before the next wave from Asia arrived, bringing with it skilled small-tool makers. Designated the Arctic Small-Tool tradition, this culture dominated arctic North America for about 1,000 years, and its members were equally at home along the coast or in the interior.

Members of the Norton and Ipiutak traditions, which flourished about 500 A.D., seemed to prefer a more coastal lifestyle. Evidence points to these people as the first to hunt whales, although they also took caribou and were skilled at fishing with seine nets.

Also about 500 A.D. the Northern Maritime tradition arose. These people became the ancestors of modern-day Inupiat Eskimos, although first their tradition had to advance through the Birnik and into the Western Thule culture. By 1200 A.D., however, the Inupiats were clearly identifiable. They lived in numerous villages in the interior, and along the rivers and coast. Villagers communicated with one another along well-developed trading routes. About this time also, dogs became pack animals for early Eskimos, who previously had pulled their sleds themselves.

Archaeologist J. Louis Giddings discovered numerous sites in the Seward Peninsula region where prehistoric man had permanent or temporary camps. While working at Cape Denbigh, north of Unalakleet, he excavated Iyatayet, uncovering signs of a people skilled in flint flaking who came to the cape seasonally to hunt caribou and seals. Giddings designated the people who had lived

Winter snow still cloaked Candle, founded in 1901 as a mining camp, in this shot taken in April 1907. (Courtesy of Thelma Rydeen Glazounow)

here members of the Denbigh Flint complex, and the Arctic Small-Tool tradition developed from these discoveries.

At Cape Espenberg, Giddings explored a series of beach ridges which yielded a record of early man spanning nearly 5,000 years. He uncovered artifacts from cultures as recent as that of the modern Inupiat and as ancient as that of the Denbigh Flint complex.

At Trail Creek caves, south of Deering within the national preserve, Helge Larsen explored a site possibly 10,000 years old where he found animal bones believed to have been handled by early man.

Western contact with the Seward Peninsula began in 1728 when Vitus Bering (1680-1741) discovered the Diomede Islands, well before his official discovery of the Alaskan mainland in 1741. In 1732 Mikhail Gvozdev and Ivan Federov landed on Big Diomede, then sailed to an anchorage off Cape Prince of Wales on the mainland. They could see the Eskimo village which lined the shores of the cape, but crew members did not go ashore. In 1767, Lt. Ivan Sindt explored the northwest coast of Alaska including the northern coast of the Seward Peninsula. Famed British explorer Capt. James Cook (1728-1779) sailed along the coast in 1778 in the HMS *Resolution,* naming King Island, Cape Prince of Wales, Cape Darby, Norton Sound and many other geographical features.

In 1816 Otto von Kotzebue (1787-1846) explored the Seward Peninsula coastline for Russia. Looking for the northwest passage, Kotzebue landed on St. Lawrence Island, then sailed north through Bering Strait and east into a large bay which he named for himself. Capt. Vasilii Kromchenko, working for the Russian American Company, discovered Golovnin Bay and the Fish River in 1821. Six years later, Fredrick W. Beechey found Port Clarence and Grantley Harbor while charting the southwest coast of the peninsula. These early expeditions led the Russian American Company to establish a trading post in 1833 at St. Michael just north of the mouth of the

Yukon, the first permanent non-native settlement near the Seward Peninsula. The opening of the post meant that each summer Diomede, King and Sledge islanders would paddle their umiaks along the peninsula's southern coast to trade with the Russians at St. Michael.

In 1848 Americans started taking an interest in the peninsula when Capt. Thomas Roys in the bark *Superior* of Long Island, New York, passed through Bering Strait and into the polar seas in his quest for bowhead whales. The *Superior* was followed in 1849 by more than 150 whaling vessels, many of which gathered at Port Clarence before trailing the ice north through the strait. All this activity led the United States government to order Navy Lt. Cmdr. John Rogers and his North Pacific Exploring

Above — The dirigible *Norge* lands at Teller after the first trans-polar flight from Europe to North America in 1926. (Anchorage Museum) **Right** — Queen of western Alaska communities, Nome matured from a crowded, dirty, gold mining tent town into a stable community with many of the amenities of urban life common in older American towns. The City Hall, built in 1904, saw many miners come and go before fire destroyed it. (Steve McCutcheon)

Expedition to survey the Bering Sea and Siberian coastlines in 1855.

Certainly one of the most important early exploring efforts in Seward Peninsula country was the overland route between Golovnin Bay and Port Clarence laid out by Baron Otto von Bendeleben in the winter of 1865-1866. The following summer Daniel Libby and his construction crew came to the shores of Grantley Harbor where they established Libbysville, headquarters for their efforts to build a telegraph line for Western Union. Their line was to be one link in a connection from Europe to North America via Siberia. By the end of winter 1867, they had surveyed 200 miles of the route and built 23 miles of telegraph line. Their efforts came to naught, however, when that summer a trans-Atlantic cable was laid, making the Western Union line unnecessary.

In 1867, the United States purchased Russian America, and the U.S. Revenue Cutter Service was assigned to maintain order in western Alaska. To fuel their ships, they set up a coaling station at Port Clarence in the 1870s. By the following decade steam whalers could winter over in Bering Sea, and in 1884 Pacific Coast Steam Whaling Company established its own coaling operation at Port Clarence.

By this time, whaling and whalers had significantly influenced the Eskimos of Seward Peninsula country. On the one hand the whalers killed walrus on which the Eskimos depended, while on the other increased trade between the two solidified the Natives' dependence on the whalers. In addition, the Eskimos had difficulty coping with the diseases and alcohol introduced by western seamen.

With the exception of the whaling crews, a handful of missionaries and prospectors were the only whites who had found their way to the Seward Peninsula. At Omilak Mountain near the Fish River valley, Eskimos had shown Capt. William Gallagher a lead-silver outcrop in 1880. Gallagher and his mining partners returned the follow-

The Rydeen family prepares for a sleigh ride in early day Candle. Almer (Slim) Rydeen was a miner, postmaster, saloon proprietor, Territorial Legislator and all-around sourdough during his more than 50 years in Alaska. His daughter, Thelma, was the first white child born in Candle. (Courtesy of Thelma Rydeen Glazounow)

Top right — One of the largest Eskimo communities on the Seward Peninsula in the 1800s, Wales was the site of one of the first missions in the region. William T. (Tom) Lopp and Harrison Thornton were the original missionaries. Eskimos murdered Thornton in 1893, but Tom Lopp went on to a distinguished career in education and reindeer management. Tom Lopp married Ellen Kittredge and their daughter Lucy was born in this mission house built in 1892. ("Annual Report on Introduction of Domestic Reindeer Into Alaska," U.S. Bureau of Education) **Right** — This unfinished monument, carved in rock, in the Nome River valley honors one of the legendary sled dog mushers, Leonhard Seppala. The Norwegian's dog teams won the All-Alaska Sweepstakes sled dog race several times, and were known for their mercy missions throughout the peninsula. One of Seppala's best known mushing exploits was his valiant effort, along with that of several other mushers, to bring diphtheria serum to Nome during a 1925 outbreak. (David Roseneau)

ing year and opened the Galena Mine. These men organized the Fish River Mining District, the first in western Alaska. The mine operated off and on for a number of years. When the mine was closed, some of the miners, rather than returning Outside, stayed in the area, opening trading posts or prospecting other valleys. John Dexter operated a post a Cheenik near present-day Golovin on Golovnin Bay. [Editor's note: The spelling of the community of Golovin and nearby Golovnin Bay differs. The Russian seaman Kromchenko named the bay for his ship, the brig *Golovnin*, which took her name from Capt. Vasilii M. Golovnin, also of the Imperial Russian Navy. The town which eventually became known as Golovin took its name from the bay but was spelled without the first "n."]

The Covenant Missionary Church opened a mission under the Rev. A.E. Karlsson in 1887, a grammar school by the end of the century and a hospital in 1920, all at Unalakleet. By 1890 William Lopp and Thornton Harrison were spreading the word among the Eskimos of Wales. The Swedish Covenant Church had a mission at Golovnin Bay, and at Port Clarence they operated a combination school and mission.

When Sheldon Jackson, pioneer missionary and educator, made a trip through the area, he concluded that the Eskimos needed a new source of protein to improve their diet. Jackson knew of the reindeer industry in Siberia and, with his encouragement, a shipment of deer disembarked at Port Clarence. Eventually, Jackson arranged for 3,000 reindeer to be imported into Alaska. [See "Reindeer," page 59.]

Gold was the catalyst which thrust the peninsula into the limelight. By 1897 word was out about the discoveries in Yukon Territory's Klondike. Hopeful miners scoured the creeks around Dawson, only to find that the good ground had already been staked. Many of these restless miners spread out across the North, looking for their own bonanza. On April 23, 1898, gold was discovered on Ophir and Melsing creeks near Council.

Children learn homemaking and shop crafts at the school at Ignaluk on Little Diomede Island. The Bureau of Indian Affairs operated elementary schools in many villages throughout the region, but students in higher grades were sent to Mt. Edgecumbe at Sitka or one of the other special high schools for Natives. (Anchorage Museum)

In September of that year, three Scandinavians found gold on Anvil Creek, near present-day Nome. Although there is debate about who actually discovered gold first at Nome, Jafet Lindeberg, Eric Lindblom and John Brynteson generally receive credit for the initial discovery. At any rate, the find led to one of the largest gold rushes in Alaska as thousands stepped onto the beaches at Nome

in the following years. [Editor's note: For details of the Nome gold rush, see *Nome, City of the Golden Beaches*, Vol. 11, No. 1, of *ALASKA GEOGRAPHIC*®. For a first-hand account of mining in the early days on the Seward Peninsula, see "A Miner Roams the Seward Peninsula," page 41.]

Across the peninsula, town after town followed the

Relics from an earlier time are strewn about this abandoned shed at the Galena Mine at Omilak, site of initial mining on the Seward Peninsula in 1881. (Mark McDermott)

As long as the gold held out, the Seward Peninsula moved headlong into the 20th century. The military, reacting to the difficulty of communicating with its Washington, D.C., headquarters and with other farflung military posts in Alaska, ordered the U.S. Army Signal Corps to build a cable and telegraph line to connect its northern outposts with the Lower 48. Work began on the Washington-Alaska Military Cable and Telegraph System (WAMCATS) section between Nome and Port Safety in the fall of 1900. The effort proceeded smoothly, and soon communities around Norton Sound were connected with St. Michael, and, by running a line across the Kaltag Portage, with the Yukon River valley settlements. By 1903 telegraph messages could be sent between Alaska and the Lower 48.

A series of mail trails, traversed by dog team in winter, connected Seward Peninsula settlements. Coastal steamers and riverboats carried the mail in weekly runs in summer. Travelers crisscrossed the peninsula along the same routes. Thelma Rydeen Glazounow, first white child born in Candle, remembers how her father mushed his dogs for weeks from this mining settlement near Kotzebue Sound on yearly trips to attend sessions of the Alaska Territorial Legislature in Juneau.

The coming of the airplane improved transportation and communication with the isolated peninsula, but it also meant the inevitable end of dog-team mail and freight service. With speed on their side . . . weather permitting, airplane pilots quickly took over the mail runs, and in the mid-1950s, the last of the sled-dog mail teams made its final run between Gambell and Savoonga.

In 1920 four military DeHavilland DH-4 planes had landed at Nome after a crosscountry flight from Washington D.C. For the next few years, pilots and planes proved their worthiness in Alaskan skies. In 1925, Noel Wien brought the first commercial flight into Nome. Two years later, he and his brother Ralph won the contract to fly mail between Fairbanks and Nome, and began

discovery of gold . . . Candle, Deering, Shelton, Solomon, Haycock, Dime Landing, Bluff. When individual prospectors either gave up or adopted some other line of work, larger mining companies consolidated their claims. With better financial backing, these companies could bring in huge floating dredges and lay out thaw fields to work the stubborn, frozen gravel.

What once had been an unknown frontier now claimed a network of small communities, led by Nome, and fueled by gold. Such an influx of miners meant that traders, bankers, lawyers and the trappings of normal community life also came to the Seward Peninsula. At first informal miners' councils kept order among the raucous miners. Later, formal government structure took over, with any lapses filled by the military.

regular scheduled service between the two communities. A mere $300 bought a one-way passenger ticket.

Perhaps one of the strangest crafts ever to fly above the Seward Peninsula landed at Teller the previous year. Roald Amundsen and Umberto Nobile brought the dirigible *Norge* down in 1926 after the first trans-polar flight from Europe to North America.

By the 1930s, peninsula residents welcomed some of the country's foremost personalities to the landing field at Nome. During their round-the-world flight in 1931, the first in airplane history, Wiley Post and navigator Harold Gatty stopped near Nome. That summer Charles Lindbergh and his wife, Anne Morrow Lindbergh, landed at Nome on their reconnaissance of the Arctic Circle route for Pan American Airways. Nome community leaders

Indians fishing through the ice at Unalakleet is how *The Illustrated London News* described this sketch of life at the Norton Sound village in the mid-1800s. (Courtesy of The Alaska Collection, Anchorage Municipal Libraries)

Boat transportation was the only way to get around Candle when the Kiwalik River flooded. (Courtesy of Thelma Rydeen Glazounow)

looked to a bright future for their town as an air crossroads, and while the peninsula certainly had its share of air traffic, it took a war to mobilize an air armada.

For years military advisors had warned of Alaska's vulnerability to attack. And if an enemy gained a stronghold on the Alaskan mainland, its planes could easily reach the West Coast. The message finally started getting through to the High Command. Well-grounded fears of Japanese attack and rumors of Russian activity near Bering Strait convinced the federal government that a military base was needed on the Seward Peninsula. Construction workers showed up in Nome in 1942, ready to build a base near the banks of the Snake River for medium- and long-range bombers and for fighters.

Taking advantage of the Eskimos' knowledge of the western Alaska environment, Marvin "Muktuk" Marston, with his headquarters at Nome, organized the Eskimos

into the Alaska Territorial Guard.

After the Japanese bombed Dutch Harbor and landed at Kiska and Attu islands in the Aleutians, residents of the Seward Peninsula waited for the other shoe to fall. Many anticipated that the Japanese would next invade the mainland, possibly somewhere on the peninsula's isolated beaches. In response, the military rushed supplies, equipment and troops to Nome.

The expected invasion never came, since Japanese activity in the Aleutians was only a diversion for the main thrust of their efforts farther south in the Pacific theater. But this did not mean that the war had passed by the peninsula. With its new air base, Nome became a stop on the route along which planes were ferried from the United States to the Soviet Union under the lend-lease program.

Bearing the brunt of German aggression on the eastern

front, the Soviet Union was short of supplies, especially planes. President Roosevelt agreed to a lend-lease program to enable allies to take advantage of United States industrial output. To get bombers to the Soviet Union, American pilots flew them from Great Falls, Montana, across Canada to Fairbanks. There Russian pilots took over the controls, flew the planes to Nome, then across Bering Strait to Siberia. Fairbanks had a larger base than Nome, and the Soviet government would not allow American pilots to fly over their territory, thus the change of pilots was made in the interior city.

After the war, the pace of life on the peninsula quieted a bit. Within a few years the military pulled back to Anchorage and Fairbanks, consolidating their forces in light of the changing concept of global conflict. Commerce returned to pre-war levels, and eventually declined even more when the price of gold made its mining uneconomical. Some Eskimos, tired of the difficulties of living in precarious circumstances, moved to Nome or Kotzebue. For the King Islanders, these difficulties were perhaps greater than elsewhere. They slowly abandoned their village on the steep-sloped island and resettled in Nome.

A similar fate befell the village of Kauwerak, formerly an important gathering place for the Kauweramiut Eskimos east of Port Clarence. Once a powerful village, most of Kauwerak's people died during the epidemics that swept the peninsula in the 1800s and early 1900s. According to Norbert Kakaruk, the survivors dispersed throughout the western peninsula, but kept their roots in the Kuzitrin River valley near Mary's Igloo. In Norbert's grandfather's time, about 400 people, mostly Catholics, lived at Mary's Igloo. When the Lutheran minister came to the area, some of the people followed him to a new village four miles away called New Igloo. During and just after World War II, the people of Mary's Igloo and New Igloo dispersed once again. Schools and stores at both communities closed, and now only a few buildings of fishing and hunting camps remain.

Tents from the mining settlement of Deering rise on a sand spit in Kotzebue Sound in September 1903. (F.H. Nowell, Photographer, Alaska Historical Library)

Solomon

About 30 miles east of Nome, the Solomon River winds down from the uplands to the shores of Norton Sound. Prospectors and dreamers came to the river valley near the turn of the century, as they did to other parts of the Seward Peninsula, hoping to make their fortune from the land or from those who worked the land.

The Solomon had felt the touch of humans centuries earlier when prehistoric man set up temporary camps at the river's mouth. By the 1800s, a small group of Eskimos who earlier lived at the junction of the Fish and Niukluk rivers, had migrated to the Solomon and established a permanent camp.

A few miners were roaming the Seward Peninsula by the 1880s; and when Tom Guarick, an Eskimo, discovered gold on Ophir Creek, hopeful prospectors headed for the area and founded the town of Council. When news of the strike reached St. Michael, miners who had been unsuccessful in the Klondike took up the quest once again, exploring the coast of Norton Sound, looking for a likely place to head inland and seek their fortune. Pierce Thomas was one of these prospectors, and in June 1899 he staked his discovery claim on the Solomon River near the mouth of Big Hurrah Creek. Three men worked the initial claim that summer, taking out $150 in gold.

By 1900 thousands of miners were poking around the creek beds of Solomon and Bonanza valleys. Miners worked placer claims on several creeks, but yields did not meet expectations. In subsequent years, mining slowly shifted from individuals with picks and shovels to operators with small dredges. Later, as hard work and low yields winnowed out the faint-hearted, survivors imported even bigger dredges.

As elsewhere on the peninsula, lack of water hindered mining efforts. To circumvent this problem, miners began in 1902 to build ditches to carry the large volumes of water needed to operate hydraulic nozzles and other equipment which could wash the gold from the gravels.

When the creek beds had been thoroughly washed and sifted, miners turned to gravel benches on the hillsides. Near Big Hurrah Creek, they discovered gold in quartz rock. T.T. Lane set about producing gold from the quartz lode in 1902. By 1904 Big Hurrah Quartz Mine had a

The dream of J. Warren Dickson, the Council City and Solomon River Railroad began here at Dickson, east across the Solomon River from the mining community of Solomon. The rail line, the first standard-gauge line in this part of Alaska, was to have run through the mountains to Council City. (B.B. Dobbs, Photographer; Alaska Historical Library)

Only a handful of folks still
live in Solomon, although
activity picks up in the
summer with fishing, hunting
and sightseeing.
(Rolfe Buzzell, Alaska Division
of Parks & Outdoor Recreation)

20-stamp mill and processed 65 to 70 tons of ore every
day.

The initial spurt of mining activity in the Solomon
valley led to establishment of a camp at Port Safety in
1899. In 1900, a store and post office opened at a camp,
known as Solomon, on a sand spit between the mouths
of Solomon and Bonanza rivers. The exposed location
left the community vulnerable to the ravages of the Bering
Sea. Thirteen years later a stormy onslaught obliterated
the townsite. Before that happened though, the town
thrived and withered, its fortunes tied to the success of
its miners. By 1904 Solomon ranked as the third largest
community on the Seward Peninsula; only Nome and
Council claimed greater populations.

The broad river valley opened a corridor to the interior.
Supply ships anchored offshore, and lighters brought the
cargo into the beach. From there, miners could move the
freight up the valley to their camps. Mail and freight
arrived by boat in summer; in winter drivers with sled
dog teams ranged the trails along the coast and inland
to Council. A well-established trail ran from Unalakleet
north and west along the coast to Nome. Solomon was
a major way station along the trail, and from here drivers
headed inland to Council.

A stage line between Nome and Council, with a rest
stop at Solomon, provided additional service in winter.
Dogs pulled the small, canvas-covered stages which ran
on runners and were heated by stoves, and dubbed the
"hot air service" by locals.

Passengers on the inland route encountered the first
roadhouse at Shovel Creek, where it served a nearby
mining camp as well as those just passing through. Ruby's
Roadhouse, 18 miles north of Solomon, was the last stop
on the route north through the mountains to Council.
Since passengers often brought word of events outside
the valley, the roadhouses served as social centers and
informal newspapers in addition to offering hot meals and
clean beds.

Moving freight overland was not cheap, however. Machinery routed crosscountry from Nome to Council could cost as much as $57.50 per ton, prohibitive in those days and a limiting factor on mining development around Council. Thus, residents welcomed the plan of Western Alaska Construction Company of Chicago to build the peninsula's first standard-gauge railroad from Solomon to Council. J. Warren Dickson, general manager of the effort, wanted his line to serve Council, Ophir Creek and Nome, as well as all the major gold-producing areas in this part of the peninsula.

Third largest community on the Seward Peninsula by 1904, Solomon had a rapid rise and an almost as speedy decline, her fortunes tied to the success of her miners. (B.B. Dobbs, Photographer; Alaska Historical Library)

35

Removing the gravel overburden from gold placer deposits required huge amounts of water. Miners built ditches, sometimes extending for several miles, to bring water from its source to their mining operations. These men and horses are part of a crew building a ditch for the Solomon River Ditch Co. in July 1904. (B.B. Dobbs, Photographer; Alaska Historical Library)

Construction began in 1903 with headquarters set up east across the river from Solomon at a site which was named Dickson. Construction activity and accompanying payroll contributed to Solomon's thriving economy. Progress during the next two construction seasons did not go as well as developers hoped. By the end of 1904 the track reached beyond Big Hurrah Creek, but was far short of anticipated schedules. Western Alaska's managers decided to open a stage line from track's end to Council. But high shipping rates, which already plagued development, soared to $66 per ton, 10 times the charge from Seattle to Nome.

Exorbitant shipping costs and slow progress on railroad construction prompted locals to encourage the Alaska Road Commission to maintain a wagon route from Nome to Council through Solomon. The commission began work on an upgraded road in 1905. The following year they helped pay for ferry service at Port Safety and Bonanza River. By 1906, with 30 miles of track laid, the railroad developers gave up. Problems with financing, lack of materials and declining revenues as a result of decreased mining activity were too difficult to surmount.

By 1907 mining activity had diminished considerably in the Solomon valley. Big Hurrah, the only lode mine in the area, shut down that year. Nevertheless, even though the number of miners and mining operations decreased, actual gold production increased because by now big floating dredges had been brought into the valley. In 1912, nine of the 31 dredges operating on the Seward Peninsula were working in the Solomon area.

As mining declined, so did the commercial centers until by 1910 Solomon and Dickson together could not muster 39 people. When the 1913 storm wiped out the Solomon townsite, survivors moved across the river to the abandoned railroad buildings at Dickson. Tom Shaughnessy, storekeeper in Solomon, reopened in Dickson in a building that became known as the Shaughnessy Roadhouse. Thus began the new community of Solomon. The

town had changed from a gold rush boomtown to a primarily Eskimo community.

In the mid-teens, W.J. "Billy" Rowe, a Nome contractor, extended his freight-hauling business to Solomon. He hauled mining equipment, built roads and in 1918 salvaged rails from the Council City and Solomon River Railroad for the Alaska Road Commission. Rowe moved an abandoned railroad building from Solomon west across the river to the base of Jerusalem Hill to serve as his headquarters and horse barn.

In fall 1918 bad luck overtook Solomon again when at least 38 residents died from the influenza epidemic which struck worldwide. Nearby villages were equally hardhit; everyone perished at Spruce Creek, an Eskimo village eight miles east of Solomon.

In 1924 Tom Shaughnessy sold his roadhouse to Pete Curran Sr., a Philadelphian and veteran of the Klondike stampede. Curran had won the contract to carry mail in winter from Unalakleet to Nome, and he bought the Shaughnessy outfit for his headquarters. Pete Jr. ran the mail from Nome to Golovin; other drivers carried the mail east around Norton Bay and down to Unalakleet. In summer Pete Jr. ran the ferry across the Bonanza River, beginning a job that would last for decades.

Except for Pete Curran Sr. and a few others, Solomon was primarily an Eskimo community whose residents lived a traditional subsistence lifestyle. The men hunted caribou, seals and beluga whales, and fished for salmon, tomcod and herring. In late fall they sought trout under the ice. Salmon caught at sea were dried for dog food; those taken inland had less oil and were eaten by villagers. Alaska Livestock and Packing Co., the Lomen Brothers' operation from Nome, hired a few residents as herdsmen for their large reindeer herd which roamed Bonanza and Solomon drainages.

In the 1930s, mining fortunes in the Solomon valley took a turn for the better thanks to the efforts of Richard and Charlie Lee. After unprofitable ventures around

Seven tons of concentrates from Big Hurrah Mine, a lode gold operation, await shipment to an Outside smelter at Mrs. Turner's Roadhouse located near the mouth of Big Hurrah Creek in the Solomon River valley. Born in Ireland in 1859, Jennie Turner operated the roadhouse after immigrating to this country in 1893. (Courtesy of Rolfe Buzzell, Alaska Division of Parks & Outdoor Recreation)

Nome, the Lees began exploring the Solomon area in 1932. In 1935 they purchased, for $500, one of the dredges that had been abandoned by earlier miners. The resurrected dredge began operating in September, and it did not take the Lees long to find out that the gold was still there in paying quantities. They quickly paid off the first dredge and purchased a second to operate farther upriver. In 1940 the two dredges scooped out more than $400,000 in gold. With this renewed activity, Solomon began to slowly grow. It remained a native community, however, with most whites living upriver.

New residents required housing, and since buildings were limited in Solomon, families began building across the river near Jerusalem Hill where Billy Rowe had his horse barn. Storms continued to plague the low-lying townsite, so in the late 1930s Pete Curran bought Rowe's property, and once again the town of Solomon was on the move. Rowe's horse barn was modified and became the new Solomon Roadhouse.

World War II dampened the mining industry throughout Alaska. Shortages of fuel, supplies and labor halted most operations. The Lee brothers, however, had stockpiled fuels and supplies just in case, and their lower dredge was the only one operating in Alaska during the war. The Lees resumed full-scale operations in 1946, but the level of general mining activity did not match pre-war efforts. In the 1950s, mining continued to decrease, and Solomon withered once again. By 1958 only three families lived in the settlement. Pete Curran died that year, and by 1959 there were not enough customers to support the store. In 1964 the Lees' dredge fell silent after 29 years.

By the mid-1980s, only a handful of year-round residents called Solomon home. Activity does pick up a bit in summer with hunting, fishing and sightseeing. And with the increased price of gold, Richard E. Lee, son of the earlier miner, is once again working his family's claims on the river.

Canvas-covered stages, heated by stoves and pulled by dogs, traversed Seward Peninsula trails when other forms of transportation were unavailable or unsuitable for the weather.
(Courtesy of Hugo Lindfors)

A Miner Roams the Seward Peninsula

By Charles O. (Otto) Steiner

Editor's note: *Unsuccessful at finding a paying lode in the Klondike, Otto Steiner came down the Yukon River and over to Nome. For years he prospected different areas of the Seward Peninsula, always seeking the rich strike that would ease his days. We thank Robert Steiner for sharing his father's notes with us.*

It is difficult to describe the confusion at Nome when we arrived from St. Michael. The beach was piled high with every kind of article. The piles stretched for miles along the shore, packed solid for a hundred feet or so, then a passageway was left just wide enough for a man to walk through, then solid piles again. Near the water's edge, men were rocking the golden sands. A man would have a cradle into which he would put a shovel of the sand, then he would add a dipper of water from the sea, then more sand. It was stated that a man often washed out $1,000 worth of gold in one day.

No official government had been established at Nome, so the citizens formed their own government and kept some order, but fights were happening all the time. Most of the trouble was over the rocking on the beach. Finally the home guards decided to allow each man to work 10 feet along the beach, and no one could trespass. There were also bitter quarrels over staking of lots. Nome lacked the order of Dawson. Most everyone felt that he was on his own and acted accordingly.

A strike was reported in Kougarok country. Four of the boys I had worked with in Dawson and Graff, whom I met on the trip downriver, decided to go there. We bought a whale boat and started west up the coast for 100 miles, then we had to turn inland for 50 miles. A small settlement called Teller had been established at the 100-mile spot at Port Clarence. Ocean storms had driven trees and logs into the bay, and the shores were lined with debris. The first thing we had to do was whipsaw lumber for a boat because the whale boat was much too large for the river.

A strike was also reported nearby which we wanted to investigate before going farther. So we gathered logs from the beach and soon had a place to sleep other than

Born in Ohio in 1865, Charles O. (Otto) Steiner came north from Washington State during the Klondike rush. Having no luck in the creeks around Dawson, he went down the Yukon and over to Nome. For years he prospected one area of the Seward Peninsula, then another. Finally, in 1911, he moved to Council to work on the Blue Goose dredge. A few years later, he married Mattie Caldwell, a teacher who was first posted to Wales, then transferred to Council. The Steiners pose here in the living room of their big house in Council in 1919.

(Courtesy of Robert Steiner)

The Blue Goose dredge scoops gravel from Ophir Creek near Council. The Blue Goose was one of the giant floating dredges that came to characterize gold mining on the Seward Peninsula after the initial rush by individual miners to work the gold placers lying on and near the surface.
(Courtesy of Robert Steiner)

the tent. After building the riverboat, two of the boys took it and went up to the Kougarok to stake claims. Graff and I stayed to report on the strike here. We found many people out at the creeks staking claims. A claim is a piece of ground 1,320 feet long and 660 feet wide containing 20 acres. Graff and I staked a few claims, but none turned out to be of much value. Graff sold his interest for $500, and I gave a lay on mine and got royalty to about the same amount.

There were two settlements on the inner shore of Port Clarence. One was Teller, and the other Bering. We happened to land at Bering. Two sisters had set up a tent and were handing out sandwiches, doughnuts and coffee.

While we were at Bering, an epidemic of measles struck the little Eskimo camp on the spit. All except one man died. I suppose the deaths were caused by the fact that when the fever got too high, the Eskimos would jump into the bay to cool off, and a few hours later they would die.

When Graff and I finally reached the Kougarok, we staked a number of claims. When we left Nome for the upper country, I bought a shotgun with which to kill birds. It proved to be worthless. One day while Graff and I were prospecting, a Native came along with six mink hides, six fox skins and six weasel skins. Graff had been in business in Chicago and was a good talker, so I told him to trade the gun for some skins. The Native first offered the fox skins, then threw in the weasel skins, but would not give more. Graff was a good horse trader though and eventually we got all of the skins for the gun.

When we came down to Nome in the fall, we were offered $15 each for the fox skins, $4 each for the mink and $1 each for the weasels. Since we were going Outside from Nome, we decided that we could get more in Seattle so we kept them. At Seattle we were offered much less than at Nome, so Graff took them to Chicago where he sold them for still less than the Seattle price. However, he got $100 for the lot, and the gun had cost me $25.

I had staked a claim on Dahl Creek which seemed to be very rich. Also I had taken a lay and an option on a claim on still richer Quartz Creek. Word had reached Nome about the strike in the Kougarok so many men wanted options. On the way Outside on the boat, three or four fellows wanted to buy my option. I could have easily sold it for $10,000, but I wanted to let my folks in on this so I refused their offers.

I interested four friends at home in Waterville, Washington, and two of them, Bill Mitchel and Ed Johnson, went with me when I returned to Nome the following spring. Feeling sure I had a bonanza up north, I sold one of my ranches at Waterville and invested in a boiler and full outfit to work my claim.

When I got to Teller the following spring, I hired two fellows to help me. We put together the knockdown boat I had bought in Seattle, and with my outfit stored in it, we started upriver. It was a hard grind for about 75 miles.

Once at the Kougarok claims, we spaded off the muck as it thawed. But when we got down to the gravel, we found that only here and there was there any gold. After working about two months, I paid off my men, weighed the gold I had taken in, and found out that with the gold and what I had left from the sale of my ranch, I could just pay all my debts. Thus was wiped out my ranch money, the $1,700 I took with me, and the optimistic view of the Dahl Creek prospect.

The $1,700 I took out with me had a tale of its own. When I got to Nome in spring 1900, I had $2,000 in Canadian $100 dollar bills. I left 17 of these with the Northern Commercial Company and took the $300 with me in smaller denominations. In the fall, when I returned to Nome, I sewed the $1,700 to the inside of my underwear, up near the breast. As everybody did in those early days, I got thoroughly lousy on the way out. When I reached Seattle, I immediately bought a new suit of underwear, went to a bathhouse and changed, throwing my old underwear in the corner. Then feeling clean once more,

I went to a restaurant. As I sat down, I remembered that my $1,700 was still sewed up in the discarded underwear. I hastened back to the bathhouse and asked for room five. Sure enough, nothing had been disturbed. The proprietor and his clean-up man followed me. "You are surely lucky. This should have been cleaned up at once. We always throw discarded clothes in the furnace."

The claim that was expected to turn out big money was the one on Quartz Creek. This is the one I had the lay and option on, and the one on which I refused all offers on the way out but sold to my friends. Bill Mitchel and Ed Johnson went with me to Quartz Creek. They had even worse luck than I did because the claim proved worthless. We could go into the shallowest still water in the creek and dig up a $5 pan now and then. In Dawson this would indicate that when a miner reached bedrock, he would find $100 pans. We all thought the same thing would happen here. But after we dammed the creek and turned all the water out, the bedrock was on the surface, not five inches down. A false bedrock. There was no way to know this until the water was out of the creek. Below this false bedrock, there was absolutely nothing. Bill and Ed cleaned up less than $100 and quit. So ended all the dreams of fortune I had for the past year.

The following winter I went down to Nome, quitting the Kougarok, and joined three fellows in a scheme to prospect on Solomon Creek, a large stream about 40 miles east of Nome. [Editor's note: See page 33.] We drove a tunnel 200 feet under a hill but found just prospects. We cut through the ice for water for our boiler and camp. One of the boys knew of a deep hole, so we dug there. The fish in this part of the stream were gathered in the pothole, probably a ton of them. They were penned in because the ice had frozen to the bottom, and there was no escape. We filled about 10 gunnysacks full of fish for our dogs. Along came a sled dog team, and the driver asked for one sack. He was on his way to Solomon at the mouth of the river. A few days later, three men passed our camp telling what a feast they had had at Solomon. The finest fish they had ever eaten. We were afraid to eat them because many had suffocated, and only a few of them showed any signs of life.

During this winter I had a hunch. I never believed much in hunches, yet many people follow them. Night after night I would dream of taking gold from my abandoned claim in the Kougarok. I concluded that the dream must have some significance, so I fixed up a sled and mushed back to the Kougarok 190 miles away.

I tried my best to justify my hunch during the next nine years. I found good money in a bench claim, but it had too much ice mixed with the gravel to thaw economically. So I dug a ditch to bring water during the summer from the head of the creek, thinking that I could sluice off the overburden as it thawed. This worked fine the first summer, but the creek miners had the first opportunity at the water, and seeing that a ditch could be dug in the frozen muck that would hold water and not thaw the banks, as had been supposed, they took the water from me. There was another stream in the area, but that water would have to be brought over a hill. So I dug another ditch, four and one-half miles long. But this ditch tapped the stream so near its head that I had water only when it rained and in the spring when the snow melted. Even so I could take out about $1,000 each summer which was all spent during the winter. After doing this for nine years, I gave up and quit the creek for good.

After my mother died, my sister Mattie, who had been living at home with our parents, came north with me. Mattie soon caught on to the way of the sourdoughs, and with rubber boots and overalls helped with the river boat taking our supplies to the Kougarok. I had built a one-room shack, and to this I added a small bedroom for Mattie. We lived here during the summer, and in the fall we moved to another board shack where the owners had stored tons of coal. The winter proved cold. We had a thermometer in the house at the head of Mattie's bed.

One morning it registered minus 40 degrees F. The house was a single board shack, and the coal fire had gone out. It was just as cold in the house as outside. During this cold weather, we wore our parkas inside, and it was impossible to keep warm unless we parked ourselves close to the stove.

In the spring, we moved back to our shack again. During this summer, Mattie married Bob Brown who owned some claims in the upper Kougarok. The U.S. Commissioner married them at Shelton, 10 miles away. Coming home we gathered a tubfull of forget-me-nots, which were in bloom along the creek, in half an hour.

During summer 1909, Bob and a few friends prospected Sweepstakes Creek. That fall 20 people embarked at Nome with about 10 tons of provisions for Sweepstakes Creek, and I joined the party. Mattie was the only woman, but she shared the hardships and fared as well as the men. We took a coastal steamer for about half of the 200-mile distance. From there we had to mush on foot, pulling a sled. We took a dog team, a horse and provisions for two years.

Ice was forming in the bay, preventing the steamer from going as far as we intended. We landed at an abandoned Eskimo camp where we stayed for two weeks until the ice froze enough to hold up the sleds. Then we mushed inland, a never-to-be-forgotten trip. The snow was six to eight feet deep, and breaking trail was difficult. To break a trail, three or four of us on snowshoes would lead, mashing down the snow as best we could. The dog team with a light load would follow, then the horse, also on snowshoes. In this way we would advance a short distance, haul up the provisions and boiler, then repeat the process. The trip took six weeks. Our thermometer, which registered to minus 60 degrees, went out of business.

One time we met a storm which stopped all travel. There was a small timber stand nearby, so we parked the horse in a tent, and made our way to the woods with the dogs. We made a fire with small saplings and piled on the wood. Soon the fire melted the snow down to the ground, and after an hour we had a space 15 feet in diameter down through eight feet of snow. We huddled here until morning. The horse fared about as badly. Snow drifted in the rear of the tent and piled up until the horse was standing almost on its head when we arrived in the morning. Most of the trail was out in the open with no trees or shelter.

Two of the men were out one day hunting for a cache of hay for the horse. Years before, a company had planned to build a telegraph line through this country and had cached hay. While looking for the hay, Frawley and Smith heard dogs barking and went to investigate. They found a man in his sleeping bag, his legs frozen stiff, two dogs dead, and three still living, but starved. The man had lost his camp ax and knife, his matches were wet, and he was lost. They brought the man, a living skeleton, to our camp. By this time we were in an abandoned cabin with snow piled up to the roof, and we were fairly comfortable. He had had no food for 10 or 12 days, had gouged out the heart of one of his dogs with a candlestick holder, drunk some of the blood, then crawled into his sleeping bag to die. We had 10 gallons of coal oil with us. We poured the oil into a washtub out in the woodshed where the temperature was about zero. We cut the sleeping bag away and put his feet in the oil. With dippers we kept pouring the oil on his legs and feet. After an hour or so, they seemed to be thawed out. The man was then sent in relays to Nome.

Not far from Trinity Creek in the Kougarok, there is a number of hot springs. This was a resort for us miners. Fish wintered here. Below the springs, the bank, heavy with grass, overhung the water. By lying on the bank and feeling along under the overhang, we could feel the fish; and the fish, since they could not see us, would lie perfectly still. By sliding a hand along the fish until the gills were reached, we could haul the fish out.

There was another hot springs, more accessible, called the Kreusemapah Hot Spring. [Editor's note: Now called Pilgrim Hot Springs.] It broke out from under the Sawtooth Range, and not many feet away another spring, this one perfectly cold, also erupted. The Catholic Mission appropriated the hot springs. They built a bathhouse and a large rooming house for visitors. At the bathhouse we could regulate the temperature by opening the valves for hot or cold water. It was a popular place for visitors from Nome and the mining region. A plot of ground nearby was subirrigated with hot water and thus remained unfrozen all winter. Here mission children raised garden truck.

On outfitting for Sweepstakes Creek, we hauled a boiler along to thaw the frozen ground. After we had established camp, we found that the ground in the creek was not frozen. We could not get to bedrock, so we prospected the bank, with poor results.

When spring came, we built a dam across the creek, turned out the water, found excellent prospects, and at one place we shoveled, we made about $6 per man per day. We prospected all summer, and in the fall went downstream about four miles where there was plenty of timber and built a log cabin. We had whipsawed enough lumber for sluice boxes, but since prospects look good, we concluded a sawmill would be advantageous. There was an abandoned sawmill at Council, 200 miles away, and Bob and I hauled it to Sweepstakes by dog team during the winter.

In spring, I decided that the prospecting we had done did not justify staying any longer. I built a small boat and started down the river for the coast, 90 miles away. Here, if I was lucky, I could get a boat to Nome. After waiting two or three days, I started along the coast in my boat, making sure to keep close to shore. When I was opposite a large stream that flows into Norton Sound, a strong wind blew me out to sea. Had the wind not slackened, I would have been blown out of sight of land. When I made it

Not much happens at Council today, but the fishing is still good as this fish camp attests.
(Roz Goodman)

back to shore, I tied up the boat and continued on foot. Small coast boats were plying along the shore, trading with the Natives. Arriving at one of the native settlements, I boarded one of the trading boats which took me to Cheenik [near Golovin] down the coast from Nome and headquarters for inland freight going up the river to Council. [Editor's note: By this time mining in the Solomon area had diminished, and the majority of freight went up the river from Golovin rather than overland from Solomon.] A number of dredges were operating at Council, and as I had now some 11 years of trying to

locate a paystreak, I concluded I would try working for wages.

At Council, I got a job as engineer and blacksmith on the steam-operated Blue Goose dredge. Whenever anything went wrong during the night, I was routed out of bed to fix it. The crank shaft broke one night; and Fred Jones, the boss, and I worked three nights and two days without stopping. We later changed from steam to gas, and there were more breaks than ever.

After some years, I went to work for Northern Light Dredge. Hughey Pearson was the dredge master, and his

wife did the cooking for the crew. These two became among the best friends I ever had. Hughey was born in Sweden, his wife was from Swedish parents in this country. After Mattie, my wife, and the children went Outside to live, I stayed with the Pearsons during spring work on the dredge.

The U.S. Commissioner at Council resigned, and I was appointed to fill the vacancy. I had to do the office work at night and the dredge work during the day. The dredge was two and one-half miles from Council, and the shift was 12 hours. Recording various papers, posting the entries and other clerical work kept me busy until 11:00 p.m. or midnight. Then in the morning I had to be on shift at 6:30 a.m.

During the winter, I enjoyed the extra work. The U.S. Commissioner recorded all papers pertaining to court procedures, issued warrants of arrest, tried all civilian cases that did not exceed $1,000, heard preliminary trials in murders and arson, prepared papers on the trials which were sent to the District Court in Nome. He also was Probate Judge, issued marriage licenses and performed the ceremonies, and did a host of clerical duties.

All freight which reached Council during the summer was ferried east from Nome along the coast of Norton Sound, then taken up the Fish River and the smaller Niukluk to the riverbank alongside Council. Horses were used to pull the riverboats over shallows; they rode along in the boats when not working. (Courtesy of Robert Steiner)

Council

By Robert Steiner

Editor's note: *Bob Steiner was born in Nome, June 22, 1917. His mother took him and his sister, Ruth, Outside in 1924. He returned in 1936 and several subsequent summers to work on the dredges. Here he describes his childhood, growing up in Council, when mining was still a major part of life on the Seward Peninsula but after the great rush of 1900.*

Alaskans refer to the Lower 48 states as Outside, probably because in the early 1900s we were locked inside our frozen fastness two-thirds of the year. We had practically no communication with the Outside — airplanes had yet to arrive in our part of Alaska. Dog teams, which came only rarely, took six weeks to reach us.

I can remember that when I was a child, my mother prepared an extensive order in early October for items to be delivered late the following June. All our clothing, other than homemade and skin garments, came from Montgomery Ward — we didn't know that Sears Roebuck existed. Food was ordered in case or barrel lots: Cases of Carnation milk, cases of peas, string beans, and other vegetables and fruits. I remember Roman Meal, Cream of Wheat and Quaker Oats, Ivory and Fels-Naptha soap, all in cases. Butter was shipped in barrels of brine. It was a glorious day when all of these provisions, and our new clothes, arrived. Dozens of back issues of *Literary Digest, Saturday Evening Post* and the Sunday edition of *New York Times* came all at once for my parents.

My mother and I returned to Council from Nome when I was four weeks old. Council was a small mining town some 70 miles from Nome. My father was engineer on the Blue Goose gold dredge operating near Council, and my mother was the town's schoolteacher.

Council was founded as a result of the first gold discovery in northern Alaska, predating the Nome strike. At one time the town had 2,000 inhabitants with a complement of saloons, hotels, stores and other businesses, even a hospital.

However, by my time, 1917, the town had dwindled

Riverboats crowd the riverbank at Council City, on the Niukluk River, first gold mining town on the Seward Peninsula.
(Ethel Becker; reprinted from *ALASKA GEOGRAPHIC®*)

to a village of perhaps 150 people, its public buildings were a general store, schoolhouse, and Arctic Brotherhood (A.B.) Hall, a two-story community house. I don't recall that there was a church in Council. Social gatherings such as dances, amateur theatricals and the annual Christmas pageant were held at the A.B. Hall. I believe it served also as a church whenever a traveling minister conducted Sunday service. I recall my parents mentioning that they were married in the A.B. Hall by a Lutheran minister using a Church of England Marriage Missal, in 1915. They lived in Council two years prior to my birth.

Perhaps, at this point in the story, I should write a bit about my parents.

My father, C.O. (Otto) Steiner, was born in Ohio in 1865, and left school after the sixth grade to learn blacksmithing, a trade that stood him in good stead in Alaska. After six years at the forge, he became, successively, a traveling book salesman, rancher (and schoolteacher in winter), steam engineer and eventually, a miner. He moved to Washington State about 1890, then up north. Like so many of the others, he never struck it rich. However, he always had a job, even during the Great Depression.

My father went originally to Dawson country in 1898, but finding no worthwhile paydirt, moved on to Nome in 1900. He worked claims in several areas of Seward Peninsula before finally settling down in Council in 1911. [Editor's note: See "A Miner Roams The Seward Peninsula," page 41.] In 1918, he left the Blue Goose and went to work for Northern Light Mining Company. He and his partners later purchased the dredge. In 1939, my father left Alaska permanently.

Mother (Mattie Caldwell Steiner) was born in Missouri in 1880 and obtained her teaching credentials at a state Normal School. After teaching in her home state, she was appointed to the school at Wales at the western tip of the Seward Peninsula. She was the only teacher for some 60 children in eight grades, and all but two of her students were Eskimos. In fact, she and the missionary family were the only white people in town. After spending two years at Wales, my mother was posted to Council.

Our schoolhouse in Council was a one-room building, serving all eight grades, and had a small enclosed entrance where, in winter, we doffed our mukluks and parkas prior to entering the schoolroom proper. As I remember, we had kerosene lamps as there was no electricity. Years later, in 1941, when I returned to Council to work for the summer, the schoolhouse was still in operation with Margaret Ulbrickson, later Mrs. Paul Maphis, as the teacher.

The number of children at the school varied — 15 to 20 normally — about three-quarters Eskimo or part-Eskimo. In winter during blizzards, one of the fathers would go from house to house collecting the younger children and tying them to a rope. At the schoolhouse, the children were released to the custody of my mother. In the afternoon, if the weather was still bad, the rope trick was re-employed.

The older schoolboys had jobs: Cutting and splitting the wood for heating the schoolhouse, building and banking the fire so the place was warm when the teacher and younger students arrived. (Winter temperatures frequently reached minus 25 degrees, and occasionally fell below minus 40 degrees.)

We had a narrow-gauge railroad at Council that ran from the scow unloading dock on the Niukluk River to the Wild Goose Mining Company camp, about 8 miles from town. The track traversed a range of hills and crossed a creek on a trestle. The railroad was built to haul supplies to the mining site, but also took passengers. The locomotive I remember was driven by a single cylinder kerosene-burning engine. I could hear its *clup, clup, clup* a mile away. I also remember a hand truck operated by pushing down on one end of a teeter-totter device connected by gears to the truck's drive wheels. I recall riding this car and the engine-driven one out to Aunty Ayers.

Aunty Ayers was the wife of Fred Ayers, superintendent of the Wild Goose dredge and a graduate in mining engineering from Stanford University. Few in Alaska, when I was a boy, had attended college. It was exciting to ride the train to his camp, and equally exciting to eat some of his wife's cookies.

The only communication in winter between Council and the big town of Nome was by infrequent dog teams since there were no aircraft. Most of the families in Council had dog teams for hauling wood, trapping and other local activities. We had no communication with the Outside for about seven months, and in Council there were no autos or other mechanized vehicles. (I did not even know the car existed until I was eight.)

But our ignorance of what went on elsewhere did not hinder our fun in our little village. We enjoyed sledding in good weather; building snowmen; having snowball fights; digging pits in the snow, covering them with a piece of crust, and waiting for the unwary to break through so we could cover him up. At school we made paper chains and doll chains for decorations, and always at Christmas the tree was loaded with items made at home or school. It was a fun life, even without radio or television, for a small boy.

Summertime was also pleasurable. We took picnic lunches up nearby Melsing or Ophir creeks and climbed over the rusty remains of mining equipment. We occasionally rode on the narrow-gauge railroad out to the Wild Goose mining operation.

One time, during spring breakup, Ruth and I and our Eskimo friend Steve were wandering over the tundra about a mile from our house. We were headed to the Wild Goose for cookies. Ruth's boot got stuck in the mud, and we could not free her. During breakup, the normally shallow creeks are dangerous, since ice jams cause the water to rise rapidly, and many people have drowned during this period. When my mother found us missing, a bell was rung to sound the general alarm, and many

of the Eskimo men in town started searching for us. My father began walking in from the dredge where he was working, some six miles away. Our tracks led down to the edge of Melsing Creek, then disappeared, and the searchers anticipated the worst. However, while I waited with Ruth, Steve started out for help. One of the adult Eskimos who was looking for us found him, and we were rescued. With our return, the school bell was rung several times to announce our safe rescue.

As far as clothing goes, everyone wore long underwear. Undergarments, sweaters, stockings, mittens and indoor footwear came from Montgomery Ward. To send for shoes, Mother drew a line around our feet as we stood on a piece of paper and sent the marked paper with the shoe order. Outdoors in summer, we wore shoe pacs, boots made Outside, with a molded rubber shoe section stitched to calf-length leather uppers. Outer clothes for men were uniformly bib overalls and blue denim shirts. Women usually made most of their clothes, as well as those of their children, from yard goods using the treadle sewing machine.

Our outer garments for winter were made by local Eskimo women. Mukluks were sealskin and reindeer hide with an insole, replaced daily, of straw gathered during the preceding summer. Our parkas were of reindeer hide, fur turned out, and lined with squirrel skin, fur turned in, and always with a facial ruff of wolverine.

In spring, we wore mosquito netting over hats; sometimes we also had netting over our beds.

Now let me describe Council life in the early 1900s. From Nome, where everything from the Outside was unloaded, transport to Council was either by water or, in rare instances, by land. Very heavy items, such as machinery, were hauled over the frozen tundra in winter on massive sleds. Since no tractors or trucks were available, teams of horses pulled the sleds. However, because of short daylight hours and frequent inclement weather, we used this system only when weight demanded.

Charles (Otto) Steiner; his wife, Mattie; Robert and Ruth pose in front of their second house in Council, the former hospital for the gold-mining town.
(Courtesy of Robert Steiner)

Townspeople brought in virtually everything during the summer. Freight was taken by coastal freighting vessels 90 or so miles to Golovin, a small trading station on a bay near the mouth of Fish River. Loads were then transferred to flat-bottom river scows, and brought upriver 40 miles to Council, on the Niukluk River, principal tributary of the Fish. Where the water was deep enough, engines could propel the scows. However, horses would drag the scows over the many gravel bars. The animals rode on the boats when not towing. Besides food, clothing, household goods, hardware and the multitude of other items necessary to keep a community going, the scows brought up barrels and barrels of oil for the dredge engines.

Travel between Council and Nome in winter, although infrequent, was not impossible. Unless delayed by storm, the trip usually took two days with a sled and good dog team. In summer, travelers made an uncomfortable trip by the same river scow and coastal vessel used for freight transport. The trip took three to six days.

Women's work in Council was varied. Primarily they were responsible for the children. One white woman acted as cook for her husband's dredge crew, my mother taught school, and all women sewed extensively. Many of the native women picked blueberries which they sold to the mining camp cooks. They also sold squirrels, rabbits and ptarmigan that they had shot. Eskimo women were accurate with their .22 rifles. They never used a shotgun because ammunition for it was too expensive, and they always shot the animal in the head to save both meat and pelts.

For men, summer was a time of constant work. Because of the short mining season, all activity continued seven days a week. Two 12-hour shifts per day usually worked the dredges, but in spring and fall the work day was reduced to a single 10-hour shift, primarily because of the lack of daylight. Incidentally, the standard pay for a day's work when I was employed there in 1940 was $8 for unskilled and $10 for skilled labor, and there was no premium for overtime.

During spring, all machinery on the dredge was inspected, repaired or replaced. This was critical because a successful four-month digging season depended on no serious breakdowns. This repair work lasted about six weeks. The actual mining season started in late June and continued through mid-October. By then we were battling freeze-up when ice formed on the dredge pond, dredge deck, and on all the cables and blocks (pulleys) associated with the dredging. When word came to shut down, workers needed about three weeks to secure the dredge for winter.

There were two skilled positions on each dredge shift, the engineer and the winchman. My father was engineer on the Blue Goose dredge. The engineer was responsible for operation of all machinery on the dredge, and the winchman handled the many levers controlling the digging of the gravel. To operate for 24 hours, a shift had to have two engineers and two winchmen. But for the 1936 season, only one trained winchman was available on the Blue Goose dredge. So my father decided to train Ed Walker, three-quarters Eskimo with a half-Russian father. Ed had gone to high school for two years and had worked two seasons in logging camps in Oregon. He proved fully competent, and later his brother Francis learned the same skill.

The mining operation took up approximately six

months of the year, a period when virtually the only activities were working, eating and sleeping. During the other six months, everyone took advantage of more leisurely pursuits. Daylight was so short that little manual work could be done, and there was no radio or TV, so we spent much time reading. Also, there was now time for serious conversation, for concerts, plays, recitations and even some original composition.

One of my favorite Alaskan poems, "Farewell to Alaska," was written one winter by Councilite Charles Snow. Here are a few lines from the first and second verses:

"O must I go out to the teeming Outside
And live like the men in the cities of pride.

Or shall I remain in this wild Arctic land
Whose big grip of freedom is clutching my hand?"

Snow, and a collaborator named Ewen MacLennan, printed their small volume of verses and presented copies to those staying in Council "as a suitable souvenir to recall the comradeship of an agreeable winter."

In addition to intellectual pursuits, we enjoyed weekly dances and outdoor activities such as ski races and dog team races.

Apart from recovering from summer's continuous work, we also had some critical chores to complete, the most important of which was cutting and hauling wood. A substantial stand of trees existed in the Council vicinity before the founding of the town in 1898. By my time though, all the timber had been cut, and we had to trek two to five miles to find firewood. Some of the more affluent families hired Eskimos to cut, split and stack their wood. Most families handled this chore as my father did.

First he built a small log cabin about five miles from Council which he could use when winter storms prevented him from returning home. On a typical day, he would leave the house in the pre-dawn darkness, ski

the five miles to his tree-cutting site, fell and limb trees for the four hours or so of daylight, then ski back home. In two or three weeks he would have enough logs for a year. Then, for the next few days, my father would hire one of the local horses to haul the logs to Council. My father had fixed up an elementary sawmill using parts from abandoned mining machinery next to our house. Using this mill, he would saw the tree-size logs into stove lengths, then split them into useable firewood with an ax.

The Eskimos that worked in Council during summer usually left for their village of White Mountain, some 15 miles to the south, for the winter. There they gathered firewood, a more time-consuming task than at Council since they had no sawmill, and trapped. Animal traps were set out over a 50- to 100-mile circuit. Every week or so, the trapper would travel along his line, removing animals that had been caught and resetting the traps. Sale of pelts produced substantial winter income.

By the time this photo was taken of the Steiner home at Council, a few trees are all that remain of a once substantial stand which grew in the area when miners first arrived at the junction of the Niukluk River and Ophir and Melsing creeks.
(Lomen Collection, University of Alaska Archives, reprinted from *ALASKA GEOGRAPHIC®*)

The Iron Horse Comes to the Peninsula

The age of the automobile had not yet hit when the first waves of miners tackled the gold-bearing gravels on the Seward Peninsula. Costs of transporting supplies and equipment to various mine sites sometimes reached $200 to $300 per ton, enough to convince miners that a more efficient and less expensive system was needed to carry weight and volume across the spongy tundra. A railroad seemed the perfect solution, and as individual miners gave way to consolidated mining companies, a system of short railroad lines was built to rich mining sites.

Charles D. Lane, president of the Wild Goose Mining and Trading Company, led the drive for the first narrow-gauge railroad on the peninsula, named, not surprisingly, the Wild Goose. Lane convinced his Board of Directors that a track to the highly profitable Anvil Creek area, where the Wild Goose company alone had taken out $21 million in gold, would bring suitable rewards. By 1900 six and one half miles of track extended from Nome to Anvil Mountain.

The Wild Goose lived up to Lane's claims, generating about $200,000 in revenue its first season. The line charged 2 cents per pound to haul freight. Round-trip passenger fare to the end of the line was $2; for 50 cents passengers could ride to Discovery on Lower Anvil Creek. Always looking for a new challenge, or perhaps his crystal ball gave him a hint of the future of gold-mining on the peninsula, Lane began selling his interests in the Wild Goose three years later. Under new ownership, the original Wild Goose became the Nome-Arctic line.

Wild Goose Mining and Trading Company also had claims near Council, north and east of Nome. Seeing how successful his first venture into the railroad business proved to be, Lane had a second Wild Goose line built to run from Council, then known as Council City, to a mine site at No. 15 Ophir Creek, about 8 miles from town. This line was also known as the Wild Goose, although officially it was the Golofnin Bay Railway Co.

Lane and the Wild Goose were not the only Seward Peninsula residents in the railroad business. J. Warren Dickson had his Council City and Solomon River Railroad, which started near Solomon on the coast of Norton Sound and was to run inland to Council but never made it

Tents for construction crew members working on the Seward Peninsula Railroad cluster at this camp near where Iron Creek enters the Pilgrim River. Several miners found paying dirt along Iron Creek and looked to the railroad to lower their freight costs.
(B.B. Dobbs, Photographer; Alaska Historical Library)

beyond mile 35. By 1903 Dickson had his crews working, at $3 a day, at the southern terminus, across the Solomon River from the mining community. By September service began, with a $1 fare taking passengers to the end of the line 10 miles out near Big Hurrah Mine. Only 1,000 feet of track were laid the following season, and to live up to its name the company established a stage line from the railroad over the mountains to Council. The final year of construction, 1906, the line reached Penelope Creek, 35 miles out. Dickson's dream never did come true, and as the value of gold production declined in the area, so did the fortunes of the railroad.

With mining activity picking up in inland reaches of the Seward Peninsula, miners in the Kougarok area clamored for cheaper freight rates. Once more promoters turned to the railroad as the answer. In 1906 the Seward Peninsula Railroad took over the Nome-Arctic track and extended the line in one season to Lane's Landing, later called Shelton, on the Kuzitrin River more than 80 miles inland, and was the southern gateway to the Kougarok.

The spongy tundra which led to unstable roadbeds on the other lines also plagued the Seward Peninsula track. Passengers never knew when they might be called on to disembark and put their muscle into hoisting the train back onto the track. But a Sunday or holiday ride to the end of the line on the Seward Peninsula was great fun. During the height of operations, two trains daily made the run. Those with light loads reached Shelton in about 12 hours. The trip could take up to 20 hours if additional cars strained the output of the locomotives.

As with other railroads on the peninsula, the Seward Peninsula's revenues declined as gold production decreased. The line had a series of owners, including the Territory of Alaska, and was taken over and rehabilitated by the federal government. The Alaska Road Commission, under federal jurisdiction, operated the line as a tram with provisions for draft animals and regulations to promote smooth traffic flow on the route. Dogs pulled many of the loads in a wide array of vehicles, many of which were known as pupmobiles. When oncoming vehicles met on the single track, rules called for lighter loads to give way to heavier ones, and always on the uphill side, so that the operator could more easily put the wagon back on the tracks.

After World War II, Charles Reader ran a rail bus on the line, which he called the Curly Q, to take tourists to Salmon Lake. By the mid-1950s, however, the Nome-Taylor Road appropriated some of the railbed for its route, and the line was no longer used as a tram.

Numerous other schemes have surfaced during the past eight decades to connect Seward Peninsula by rail with the rest of Alaska and the entire continent. Some even envisioned a tunnel under Bering Strait and a rail tie across Siberia to Europe. Although the promoters thought big, the realities of distance, topography and finance curtailed their dreams.

Today scattered remnants of rolling stock and tracks lie in the tundra, reminders of a time when railroads were seen as the solution to transportation problems for isolated mining camps on the Seward Peninsula.

Rolling stock from the Council City and Solomon River Railroad lies scattered across the tundra near Solomon east of Nome. The southern terminus for the line was Dickson, east across the Solomon River from the mining town.
(John & Margaret Ibbotson)

Reindeer

By Bill Sheppard

Editor's note: *While surveying archaeological sites in the Bering Strait region, Bill Sheppard was able to put his background in anthropology to work by interviewing many of the old-timers who worked in the early days of reindeer herding.*

It is no exaggeration to state that most residents of Seward Peninsula have had some involvement with reindeer herding during their lifetimes. In many ways, this introduced industry has had far-reaching effects equal to those of the gold rush on the people of this area.

The introduction of reindeer to Seward Peninsula began as the result of efforts of Dr. Sheldon Jackson, General Agent for Education in Alaska. Jackson believed that seriously depleted stocks of whales, walrus and caribou threatened the Eskimos with starvation and extinction. Reindeer, he proposed, could provide an alternative and more stable food source. But Jackson wanted to do more than save the Eskimos from starvation; he wanted to embark on an ambitious program of cultural change. In his words, reindeer herding would "do more than preserve life — it will preserve the self respect of the people and advance them in the scale of civilization." It is now believed that Jackson's pessimistic prediction was rooted in culture shock and a misunderstanding of Eskimo culture. Nevertheless, the idea did take root and changed the lifestyles of Seward Peninsula people.

Initially, Jackson had no success in securing government support for his project, but with private funds he was able to purchase 171 Siberian reindeer during summer 1892. The deer were brought ashore at Port Clarence, where Teller Reindeer Station was established. The following year, Congress appropriated the first funds for the reindeer project. Between 1892 and 1902, 1,280 reindeer were transported from Siberia before Russia banned further exports of the animals.

The reindeer herding project expanded rapidly in succeeding years. Under a program of apprenticeship, Eskimos were taught reindeer husbandry and, during a

A Lapp woman milks reindeer. Laplanders, experienced at herding reindeer in their Scandinavian homeland, were brought to Alaska to teach the Eskimos how to handle the domestic deer.
(*Annual Report on Introduction of Domestic Reindeer Into Alaska,* U.S. Bureau of Education)

period of two to five years, earned deer to start their own herds. At first, the government tried to employ Siberians to teach the Eskimos, but when this quickly proved a failure, partly because of the traditional animosity between Siberians and Alaskans, Lapps from northern Scandinavia were brought to Seward Peninsula in 1894. The Lapps were more successful as teachers, but the majority later found the gold fields more attractive than the reindeer range.

Three years after the reindeer arrived at Teller, the first Eskimo was given a herd to manage independently. Charlie Antisarlook received 115 deer, which he moved to the Sinuk River, west of modern-day Nome. As with other subsequent loans of reindeer, officials intended that Antisarlook should nurture and expand the herd for several years, after which he would pay back the loan and keep the increase. No sooner had Antisarlook paid

back his original loan of deer, than the remainder of the herd was borrowed and herded northward to provide meat for whalers stranded near Barrow. Charlie later perished in the 1900 measles epidemic. Mary, Charlie's wife, inherited the herd and, after moving to Unalakleet, became well known as "Sinrock Mary, the Reindeer Queen."

The expansion of reindeer herding on Seward Peninsula was so rapid that by 1914 all grazing land in the region had been divided up between nearly 30 separate herds. Yet while reindeer herding was booming, the local markets it depended on began to dry up as the pace of mining operations slackened. To cope with this and other problems, the government encouraged herders to form associations. By 1930 virtually all Eskimo herds had been combined into cooperative village herds.

While the Eskimos were trying to solve their problems

through cooperative ownership, another factor emerged that greatly affected later events. In 1914, the Nome-based Lomen family began buying reindeer. On Seward Peninsula, the Lomens purchased mission herds at Teller and Golovin, as well as those of two Laplanders. This non-Native venture expanded to the point where, in one year, the Lomens sold more than 14,000 carcasses. Tensions mounted between the Lomens and the Eskimo herders and their supporters. This conflict culminated in the passage of the 1937 Reindeer Act that prohibited non-Native ownership of reindeer. The lobbying efforts of advocates for native rights such as C.L. Andrews played an important role in enactment of this legislation; but records also suggest that Lower 48 cattlemen, hard-pressed by the Depression and threatened by Lomen competition, also influenced Congress to pass the legislation.

Ironically, despite elimination of the Lomens and other white competitors from the scene, Eskimo reindeer herding went through a period of catastrophic decline in the late 1930s and early 1940s. By 1951, just 6,500 reindeer were left on Seward Peninsula, less than six times the number originally imported 60 years earlier. During this period, reindeer herding was reorganized, with the government aiding in the re-establishment of small, individually owned herds.

From its low point in the 1940s, Seward Peninsula reindeer herding has experienced a slow resurgence. Today, more than 16,000 reindeer from a dozen herds roam the region. While the sale of meat still accounts for most of the revenue from herding operations, about one-third of the total income comes from the sale of antler. The velvet-covered antler of adult deer, which may fetch $20 per pound or more, is sold in the Far East where it is believed to cure a variety of disorders.

The future of Seward Peninsula reindeer herding appears bright. At present, the demand for reindeer meat, both within and outside the region, outstrips production.

The more exotic antler market, while affected by a developing antler industry in New Zealand, has remained stable for several years. No doubt Sheldon Jackson would be surprised by the nature of Seward Peninsula reindeer herding nearly 100 years after its inception, but he would surely be pleased with the positive contribution herding makes to the region's economy today.

Reindeer carcasses are wrapped in stretchable mesh game bags so air can circulate around the meat. (Allen Marquette)

61

St. Lawrence Island

As Timeless As The Seasons

By Charlie Crangle

Editor's note: *Charlie is in his second year as a teacher at Savoonga and is compiling a resource library for students on St. Lawrence Island.*

Imagine a place in the middle of an ocean which is frozen six months of the year, a place where the International Dateline takes a jog to the west to keep the island in the same day as the rest of the country. Imagine a place where a proud people, bound to a subsistence lifestyle in a harsh, subarctic climate, cling to their cultural heritage despite the advent of modern amenities.

There exists such a place. St. Lawrence Island, of volcanic origin, rises from the northern Bering Sea about 165 miles southwest of Nome. One hundred miles long and twenty miles wide, the island is home to a Yupik culture which, because of the island's isolation, is still intact. The Siberian Yupik language is spoken only here and among Siberian mainlanders. Siberia is far closer than mainland Alaska and prior to this century, the majority of the islanders' contact was with the Siberians.

Decimated by disease and famine in the 19th century, the islands' once large population is now centered in two villages. The 500 villagers of Gambell, on the west end of the island, can easily see the Siberian mountains, a scant 38 miles away across Bering Strait. Slightly larger than Gambell and located on the island's north shore, Savoonga is known as the "Walrus Capital of the World." Both villages share ownership of the island's roughly two and one-half million acres, land the Natives received title to as a result of provisions of the Alaska Native Claims Settlement Act (ANCSA) of 1971.

Government in the villages reflects the situation left in the wake of ANCSA. There are three governing bodies; the IRA Council, city government and the village corporation. The IRA Councils, formed by the Indian Reorganization Act of 1936, predate the other two forms of local sovereignty. ANCSA mandated the other two forms. Village corporations were created to administer the newly titled lands, and local city governments were formed to execute municipal laws and provide services as determined by the state.

Junior Slwooko harpoons a bowhead whale. When one of these huge, slow-swimming behemoths is taken, the entire village shares in the bounty. (Chlaus Lotscher)

An Eskimo woman splits a walrus hide with an ulu. The walrus is the mainstay of the St. Lawrence Islanders' subsistence economy. Its hide is used in a variety of ways including to cover the wood frame of a skin boat. In years past, walrus hide provided the roofing for the villagers' houses.
(Chlaus Lotscher)

Both Gambell and Savoonga have airstrips capable of servicing four-engine cargo planes. Gambell's strip is paved and was built originally by the military during the 1940s. Savoonga's strip was built in the late 1960s. Prior to that, mail was carried from Gambell to Savoonga once a week by dog team in the winter, and less frequently by boat in summer. Today, mail is delivered to the island daily by scheduled air service from the mainland. There are currently three passenger flights and two weekly scheduled air cargo flights serving Gambell and Savoonga. These weekly cargo flights enable the stores in the villages to use "by-pass" mail to lessen freight costs. "By-pass" mail, offered by the U.S. Postal Service, is far cheaper than paying full freight where air freight charges in late 1986 were $.99 per pound from Anchorage.

Air freight service has dramatically increased variety in the village stores. While costs are obviously higher than in communities served by road or rail, selection is excellent and prices fair considering the island's remoteness. Below are some sample prices at Savoonga's Native Store in late 1986:

1 pound Folgers coffee	$6.15
5 pounds cheddar cheese	$25.59
10 pounds white flour	$5.59
small can Campbell's tomato soup	$.85
small head lettuce	$1.29
6 cans Coca Cola	$4.50
6½-ounce can tunafish	$2.45
1 gallon gasoline	$2.00
1 gallon stove oil	$1.65

Stores on St. Lawrence Island are truly "general stores" where shoppers can purchase everything from snow machines to kiwi fruit. Despite the convenience and variety of the community stores, some villagers choose to order from catalogs to save money. However, everyone depends on the village stores for fresh and frozen items.

Neither village has a water or sewer system to serve individual homes. A centrally located washeteria provides shower and laundry facilities in each community. Most people haul water daily to their homes from conveniently spaced outlet taps off the main water line. All homes in the villages use honeybuckets. The waste is picked up daily and disposed of in a city landfill. Preliminary work to install indoor plumbing into many of the village houses is under way in Savoonga. In the future, villagers from both communities can expect to no longer have to haul water.

The economies of both villages are a mix of subsistence, subsidies and cash. Cash is generated from a limited number of government and service jobs. The majority of the remaining cash flow stems from sale of ivory carvings or skin-sewn products.

Activity in the island's communities focuses on the land and the surrounding sea, regardless of the season.

Telltale signs of a subsistence lifestyle, birds, fish and meat hang to dry alongside this home in Gambell.
(Chlaus Lotscher)
Blood drains from braided seal intestines, another subsistence food for St. Lawrence Islanders. When the intestines are dry, they are cut into slices and either eaten raw or boiled.
(Chlaus Lotscher)

An Eskimo hunter cuts up a ringed seal carcass on the Punuk Islands off the southeast coast of St. Lawrence. (Kevin Schafer) Walrus meat is sewn inside a pouch of walrus hide for storage in a permafrost cache at Gambell. (Chlaus Lotscher)

Islanders celebrate Fourth of July with patriotic enthusiasm, and the holiday truly marks the beginning of summer. During this season, most people travel to their family camps which are scattered along the island's coast. While at camp, the islanders fish, boat, hunt marine mammals and seabirds, gather greens and seafoods, collect bird eggs from numerous nesting colonies and pick berries — much as their forefathers have done for thousands of years. Beyond these traditional activities, a relatively new pastime has sprung up that is, paradoxically, still tightly woven to the past.

Digging for old ivory and artifacts, buried for generations in old village sites around the island, has become a popular and lucrative summer pastime. Wealthy collectors from off island covet St. Lawrence Island artifacts. In addition to valuable artifacts, many of the digging sites yield assorted pieces of old ivory. These are transformed into delicate carvings or sold outright to ivory traders. Law prohibits non-Natives from purchasing raw, unworked ivory. As a consequence, white carvers and scrimshaw artists in faraway cities have created a demand for old

ivory, which can be bought and sold legally in its raw state.

Fall on St. Lawrence brings rapid changes; winds increase and storms are more frequent. The seabird colonies are abandoned abruptly by mid-September with birds often flying south through gale driven snow to escape to warmer climes. Islanders return from camp and hurry to complete summer building projects and food gathering before the weather turns to the dominant season . . . winter. Outside, snow geese, eiders, Canada geese and cormorants hang to dry alongside salmon and grayling.

Schools bustle as children fresh from a summer at camp return to class. A three-wheeler rushes by with a freshly killed seal balanced on the back; family freezers are packed with foods gathered during the brief, hectic harvest. Last efforts at ivory digging continue at sites close to the villages until the ground freezes. Autumn is short, and by October snow blankets the villages, with bare ground not to be seen again until June.

By November, snow machines have supplanted three-wheelers as basic village transportation and shore ice begins to form. Indoor activities which have suffered from poor attendance during summer and early fall suddenly see a rebirth in popularity. Bingo is played several times a week. Village coffee shops bustle with activity until early morning hours. High school basketball and wrestling seasons are soon in full swing with contests well-attended, especially those for island bragging rights between the Gambell King Polar Bears and the Savoonga Siberian Huskies. Community education, dances, city league basketball, community college courses, card playing and visiting are other popular indoor pastimes. The island is icebound by December, and daylight is reduced to about four hours. In spite of this, when the weather is clear, activity shifts back outside as islanders hunt for seals and jig for tomcod and blue crab.

Village schools are the center of Christmas season celebrations. Christmas programs are held each year in either the churches or schools and feature plays, skits and

Each summer, Eskimo families head for hunting and fishing camps around the island where they gather food for the long winter.
(Chlaus Lotscher)

caroling by the children, many of whom are dressed in traditional garb: Sealskin parkas, mukluks and even polar bear pants. These are usually standing-room-only events, highlighted by a visit from Santa. Following the program, villagers exchange gifts.

After the holiday season, the focus returns to traditional hunting with arrival of polar bears and the corresponding slow increase in daylight needed to hunt them. Because of its location, St. Lawrence is visited by the largest male bears, powerful swimmers who spend the majority of their time amid the ice floes of the open ocean, far from land. By February, successful hunters from both villages have a number of hides hanging outside, curing in the subarctic air.

March soon arrives, and with it lengthening days. The islanders turn their thoughts to the spring whale hunt. Women sew thick, tawny walrus hides into *angyaqs* (skin boats), in a fashion reminiscent of a New England sewing bee. Signs in the stores announce meetings for whaling captains. Harpoons are sharpened and tested. Savoonga villagers hunt on the island's south side. Much of March is spent gathering supplies and shuttling them by snow machine and sled to whaling camp. It is quite a spectacle to see the large *angyaqs* hauled through town on sleds on their way to whaling camp. In Gambell, unlike Savoonga, migrating bowhead whales pass by in waters just to the west of the village. Whaling crews use their villages as a base and do not have to travel to distant camps.

May's warmer temperatures mark the end of whaling, and open leads in the pack ice signal the beginning of yet another important hunt. The walrus season is brief, and villagers must capitalize on what little favorable weather and ice conditions they get during the walrus migration. After a successful hunt, aluminum skiffs with outboard motors return to the village full of fresh slabs of walrus meat and heads with white tusks. If the season is productive, the signs are everywhere. Meat racks are

Above — Walrus stomachs, meticulously scraped and cleaned, are blown up and hung to dry. When dried, they are made into drums. (Chlaus Lotscher) **Right** — Born in Siberia, the late Pauline Appassignok wears the facial tattoos of her people, the Siberian Yupik. (Chlaus Lotscher)

soon full with food again. Heavy walrus heads lie balanced outside houses, their massive incisors jammed into snowbanks. Villagers share their take among friends and relatives. No one is left without. The school year ends during the walrus hunting season, and the subsistence life cycle begins again. This is a joyous time of year. There is ample food, and villagers look forward to a fruitful summer of traditional activities. *Upenghaq* (springtime) has returned to St. Lawrence Island, a place in transition, yet still clinging to its proud heritage steeped in traditional subsistence hunting.

St. Lawrence islanders today value their land and the sea surrounding it more than ever. While some of today's modern conveniences make life a bit easier, the island environment provides them with the means to continue their traditional way of life just as it has for thousands of years. Their culture and their language reflect the strength they derive from their aboriginal lands. In a harsh climate, it takes dedication to thrive, but the land and the sea have always provided for those who have toiled here. Season by season, the ancient pulse is still steady and strong.

Much of the St. Lawrence Island coastline is similar to Kongkok Bay, shown here, 27 miles south of Gambell on the island's west coast. At least 1.2 million least and crested auklets nest in Kongkok Basin which flanks the lagoon and bay. (David Roseneau)
These whalers sail their skin boat through drift ice off St. Lawrence Island.
(Chlaus Lotscher)

St. Matthew and Hall Islands
Oasis of Wildness

By Elaine Rhode

Editor's note: *A freelance biologist and writer, Elaine has spent several seasons exploring the islands of the Bering Sea.*

Wind, the only sound. Then voices, hundreds of thousands raised in cacophony. Not the voices of humans but the guttural mutterings and high-pitched laughter of birds wheeling in the air, bobbing on the ocean and clinging to sheer volcanic cliffs. The islands of St. Matthew, Hall and Pinnacle rise as an oasis from the middle of the Bering Sea 375 miles southwest of Nome and 200 miles south of St. Lawrence Island.

Few human voices ever echoed from here. Until 1980 less than 30 known expeditions into this wild expanse of ocean have come near enough to sight these islands, and only half of those expeditions spent more than a day or two ashore since Russian explorers drew "I. Apost. Matthei" on a map in 1767.

No one in historic or recent times has lived here per-manently. There are no harbors, no landing strips, no towns. These islands are the last large wilderness islands in the Bering Sea.

The few human visitors reaching this wilderness have brought back tantalizing tales of its animal residents, some so unique or abundant as to make the islands famous in natural history circles. For most, however, the islands only tease from afar.

When an offer came to join a scientific team making a wildlife survey of the islands, I jumped at the chance to see them myself. The U.S. Fish and Wildlife Service sent eight of us to this unit of the Alaska Maritime National Wildlife Refuge. We would make two temporary base camps on the largest island, 32½-mile-long St. Matthew, and study everything around us for the next three months.

We first tried to land on May 15, 1982, but thick ice stopped our ship 60 miles to the south. A week later, as we gazed at the snowy profile of St. Matthew and prepared to land, we wondered if we would meet a wandering polar

On a rare clear day, Cape Upright looms above the Bering Sea, its 1,505-foot summit the highest point on St. Matthew Island.
(Elaine Rhode)

This crested auklet is one of the millions of seabirds which nest on the cliffs of St. Matthew Island. President Theodore Roosevelt originally made the island group a preserve in 1909 to protect its native birds.
(Kevin Schafer)

bear. These islands have a long history of resident polar bears.

When the first recorded expedition to go ashore drew near Hall Island on July 14, 1791, several white bears "swam round the ship while we were at anchor, and three of them made many attempts to get up the ship's side; but at length they all swam to the large (St. Matthew) island," wrote the expedition historian.

That incident began more than 100 years of summer encounters with polar bears apparently breeding on the islands. Whalers began calling them the "Bear Islands" and soon they became known as the only place in Alaska to see polar bears in midsummer.

Henry Wood Elliott, noted scientist making the first studies of northern fur seals on the Pribilof Islands 230 miles to the south, made a special trip in 1874 to see the bears.

Elliott remembered: "An old Russian record prepared us in landing to find bears here, but it did not cause us to be equal to the sight we saw, for we met bears, yea, hundreds of them. During the nine days that we were surveying this island we never were one moment while on land out of sight of a bear or bears."

Elliott believed his party to be the first to study the islands, and the first to set foot on them since the winter of 1810-1811 when he recorded that an ill-fated party of five Russians and seven Aleuts, probably from the Pribilofs, wintered on the islands to hunt polar bears. Four of the Russians died of scurvy and the rest barely escaped alive.

Elliott estimated his party saw no less than 250 or 300 bears during the nine days. He and his party shot 15 to 20 of the bears but found their summer coats to be shedding. Bear meat, however, he described as excellent.

Eleven years later, on September 8, 1885, four polar bears were on the beach when a hunting party from the steamer *Corwin* of the U.S. Revenue Service went ashore. Three bears escaped over the hills under cover of fog,

but the largest took refuge in the boulders where it was killed by Charles Townsend, a Smithsonian Institution naturalist.

Thereafter the mists of uncertainty obscure the fate of these island polar bears. Another scientific expedition saw some in 1891; the *Corwin* returned and her crew shot 16 bears; but in 1899 when the Harriman Expedition landed, the polar bears "which our sportsmen had hoped for were not found." In 1916 well-beaten trails of bears were still clearly visible across the tundra, but only skulls were found, all with bullet holes in them.

Tracks of a bear were seen in winter, 1942-1943, and one bear was spotted on St. Matthew in March 1976, but never again have the white bears made the islands their year-round home.

What happened? Alaskan polar bear biologists have proposed that the animals may have been of separate stock, bonded to the islands. When the original clan was wiped out, that bond was erased. Bears that might have repopulated the islands were so heavily hunted in succeeding years that the opportunity was lost.

Visitors can walk today in the fading trails of the polar bears. I followed one of those ghostly paths along a cliff top to an overlook above a beach filled with walrus.

Herds of walrus, Elliott and other scientists concluded, attracted polar bears to the islands. The 1791 Billings-Sarychev expedition that first told of sighting the bears on these islands also found walrus and their skeletons. Many accounts since that time note the presence of walrus.

A St. Matthew singing vole, found nowhere else in the world, chomps on some of the lush vegetation which carpets suitable soil on the remote island.
(David Roseneau)

73

Right — If the Japanese had invaded St. Matthew Island, this .30-caliber machine gun would have met them. The only "enemy action" came in May 1943 when an aircraft sighting turned out to be a flock of migrating waterfowl. (Ben Schlegel; courtesy of Elaine Rhode) Below — Jacob Stalker joined the St. Matthew soldiers as their survival instructor. Born in the Noatak region, Stalker made his own skis from driftwood as his father taught him, hunted seals and birds for the camp, and gathered much of the driftwood for heating when their coal supply washed out to sea. (Ben Schlegel; courtesy of Elaine Rhode)

My first views of walrus came soon after I arrived. Five walrus bobbed at rest offshore, floating in a cluster with their heads and tusks up out of the water.

For days we continued to see rafts of walrus cruising past our camp without finding the beach where they would haul out, or come ashore to sleep. When the ice moved north and a day dawned calm, we motored around the southern end of St. Matthew in our rubber boat. We saw no walrus as we rounded Cape Upright. But then, below the last cliff face, huddled 20 walrus on a narrow beach under a snow cornice.

The next day storm surf washed the beach, and the walrus were gone. By the following day the snow cornice had avalanched, making the beach inaccessible until it melted. Despite these temporary setbacks, we observed

Ten men arrived on St. Matthew Island in September 1942 to build the first wartime outpost and live there without mail or supply drops until they were relieved the following summer. Back row from left: John McRae, Jake Oleynik, Harry Lyons, Lynn Watt, Ray Pemberton; front row: Ben Schlegel, Jacob Stalker, George Ruef. (Not pictured: Robert Garr and John Blue.) (Ben Schlegel, courtesy of Elaine Rhode)

With a partner, Ben Schlegel took weather readings every six hours while on the island, and a team of two radio operators transmitted the coded data to fill an information gap in the Bering Sea war zone. (Ben Schlegel; courtesy of Elaine Rhode)

New walruses joining an
already crowded resting
beach take their time in
approaching so as not to
draw attacks from the beach
masters. (Elaine Rhode)

from 6 to 158 walrus basking in the 40-degree temperature on the beach most days of summer. On rare days when the sun burned away all traces of fog and the temperature rose, the walrus deserted the beach.

Only loafing males spend their summers in the vicinity of these islands. Females are north, following and using the ice as safe birthing areas and nurseries to raise their calves.

The social etiquette for walrus coming ashore is comical to watch. If there are only a few animals on the beach, an incoming walrus might cruise just offshore, waiting for other recruits. If the beach is packed, a newcomer slowly heaves himself into the shallows, scratches or looks away, all the while seeming quite aloof with no aggressive intentions. Inch by inch he moves toward the prone crowd, stopping if one of the sleeping bulls lifts his head in threat.

Then deserting caution, he clambers atop the bulls

76

nearest shore, waking up those being squeezed under him. Depending on relative tusk size, the newcomer either forges ahead or changes course. The ideal location seems to be in the middle of the heap. Younger, smaller walrus get stuck with the edges and near shore where the two-foot tide or surf might cool them.

Now the walrus begins to blush. The longer he remains on shore, the warmer and drier — and pinker — the hide becomes. Blood vessels constricted in icy water to conserve body heat are now expanding with a rush to help regulate changing body temperature.

As I sat watching, a tiny, almost all white bird flitted over the slumbering sea giants and landed on a hummock in the bank above them. A McKay's bunting.

St. Matthew and Hall islands cradle almost the entire world population of McKay's bunting in summer. No one

Far left — The Mongolian plover is one of more than two dozen species of birds from Asia that visit the refuge during migration each year. (Elaine Rhode) **Left** — A young McKay's bunting, just out of its rock-cave nest, waits for its busy parents to return with insects. Virtually all of the world's McKay's bunting population nests in the St. Matthew group. (Elaine Rhode)

77

Above — Northern fulmars and arctic foxes hunting them are often in the clouds as the mountain tops of St. Matthew Island gather their own weather from the fog-cloaked Bering Sea. (Elaine Rhode)

Right — After raiding a cliff ledge of seabirds, an arctic fox runs home to its den of hungry pups with a murre egg held unbroken in its mouth. (Elaine Rhode)

Far right — Perhaps the best known of Alaska's seabirds, the horned puffin finds the isolated cliffs of St. Matthew suitable habitat for digging its burrows. (Kevin Schafer)

realized the bird existed until 1879, and not until 1885 did someone discover that these islands were its exclusive nesting place.

In early October, McKay's buntings migrate barely a few hundred miles east, trading the harsh winter on St. Matthew and Hall islands for the only somewhat less austere weather and greater opportunity for food on Alaska's western mainland.

Male McKay's buntings are white with dabs of black on wing tips and tail. Females also have fine streaks of gray on their backs and heads. The closest relative, the snow bunting, wears solid black on its back and more black on its wings and tail. It breeds around the world in the coastal Arctic and in winter wanders as far south as the northern Lower 48, Japan and France.

Once the snows melt, the flash of white of the McKay's bunting is strikingly conspicuous over its realm. We found it nesting deep in rock rubble on mountainsides, in deserted vole holes along stream banks and in crevices of cliff faces above the ocean. When the chicks finally left their dark nurseries in late July, the adults still followed them with beaks filled with insects.

On the sea cliffs a similar drama is being enacted a million times over. The stars are seabirds — birds most people never see because they live on the ocean, not just pass over it en route to somewhere else. When the need to reproduce sends them in search of a nest site, seabirds choose remote, barren rocks with more vertical than horizontal space. St. Matthew, Hall and Pinnacle islands have fit that description for thousands of years.

Seabirds need nothing from the islands except a flat ledge, crevice or earth burrow for nesting; they continue to feed in the sea and, in the case of murres, take their offspring back to the ocean even before they can fly.

The islands lie near the western edge of the shallow continental shelf and between gyrating ocean currents. The Bering Sea provides something for every palate. To the northwest are high concentrations of bottom dwelling organisms such as worms, snails, barnacles and shrimp-like crustaceans. Waters to the south are especially rich in animal plankton. Both feed the fishes living at the edge of the continental shelf.

In spring the sea around St. Matthew, Hall and Pinnacle islands is dotted black with returning birds. More than two million, and perhaps as many as five million, nest here.

Early accounts of the huge numbers of seabirds on the islands filtered back to Washington, D.C., where in 1909 President Theodore Roosevelt designated the islands a Bering Sea Reservation "as a preserve and breeding ground for native birds." With three other seabird reservations named that same year, the islands became the charter national wildlife refuges of Alaska. In 1970 Congress gave the refuge additional status as an official national wilderness area.

The Bering Sea refuge is the most northerly nesting site for the northern fulmar. White and gray with an unusual tubed bill for ridding its system of excess salt, the fulmar feeds by gliding just above the waves and scavenging from the surface. Virtually all two million of Alaska's fulmars breed in four locations including the St. Matthew group.

Each year about half a million fulmars set up territories in barren niches on the vertical faces of Pinnacle, Hall and St. Matthew islands.

Near them, on slightly wider ledges, are common and thick-billed murres. The islands accommodate nearly a million murres, nesting in greatest abundance on the sheer headlands of Hall Island.

Black-legged kittiwakes can be found on the lower portions of cliffs. Unlike fulmars and murres, kittiwakes make a nest instead of laying their eggs on bare rock. During courtship, the birds fly inland to the muddy shores of ponds to gather mud and grass. Back on the cliff face they paste the mixture onto a jutting rock and build up a nest platform, tamping the final cup shape with their webbed feet.

Auklets and puffins choose to nest out of the weather. Parakeet auklets and horned puffins squeeze through any crack that opens into an interior chamber to lay their eggs. Tufted puffins prefer gentler slopes that have some soil covering them so they can dig burrows. The tiny offshore islet of Ghost Seal Rock is pockmarked with more than 500 burrows.

The highest mountain peaks on St. Matthew and Hall islands have areas of old rock slides where half a million least and crested auklets nest. I climbed over the 1,505-foot summit of Cape Upright and down into its auklet bowl to witness a special sight. Morning, noon and evening when one half of the pair returns from fishing at sea to feed or relieve its underground mate, the mountainside turns into a giant beehive.

We followed the nesting progress of the different seabirds and eagerly checked each day to see if the pelagic

Left — A biologist hikes the grass-covered, rocky slopes of northern St. Matthew Island heading for Bull Seal Point, in the middle distance. (David Roseneau) **Above** — Hall Island, seen here from Glory of Russia Cape, is the second largest island in the St. Matthew group. Named Walrus Island by early Russian hunters, the English recorded the five-mile-long island as Hall, perhaps for a crewman sailing with Capt. Joseph Billings, one of the first to arrive at the island group. (David Roseneau)

cormorants still had four youngsters and if any kittiwake eggs had hatched. Every stage from incubation through the first winter at sea stands as a hurdle to the success of a summer's breeding and the survival of a chick. Chances for failure are many: Loss to predatory foxes and gulls; landslides or storms; death of one of the adults; or poor fishing out at sea.

Arctic foxes are the most visible threat. Enterprising trappers introduced foxes to many Alaskan islands to farm their furs, but the arctic foxes of St. Matthew and Hall islands are native. Sometime in the past, foxes merely walked across the winter ice onto the islands and stayed.

My second evening at St. Matthew I saw proof of the fox's ice walking skill. Without pause, a fox ran from the beach and onto the pancakes of ice moving around Cape Upright. The fox trotted from floe to floe, never hesitating at the gaps, moving first out to sea then paralleling the coast until out of sight. Suddenly it reappeared within six feet of me as I stood in a cleft at the base of a sea cliff.

We put colored ear tags on as many foxes as we could live-trap. The majority were bachelors or at least without families and tended to pass near camp often since, unknowingly, we had set up camp on a main fox highway to the seabird cliffs and auklet colony of Cape Upright.

One male and female, seeming to be paired but without pups, claimed our camp as their turf. Another pair, also without pups, lived by the lake to our side.

This phenomenon of paired but not breeding foxes may be due to competition for den sites where the older, higher status animals get the choice dens. Those sites were in the heart of seabird colonies where "the livin' is easy" during the high stress period of raising pups. Two dens we found in marginal habitat — beach driftwood piles far from seabird cliffs — kept losing pups and were left with one runt each by August. Such den sites may be viable only in years when the islands' only other land mammal, a meadow vole, is abundant.

A den I found in the summit of a dense seabird colony had at least four pups and was littered with remains of murres, horned puffins, crested auklets and northern fulmars.

We learned never to underestimate the agility of arctic

foxes as we watched a fox picking its way along bird-filled cliff ledges we thought no fox could reach. Looking for eggs, it chased fulmars off their nest sites and carried off the egg of one of our study pairs, then came back for a second. In the meantime, glaucous gulls swooped in to take two eggs from untended nests where birds had been frightened away by the fox. The fox returned once more, grabbed another egg, and carried it unbroken in its mouth straight up an avalanche chute still filled with snow.

During spring breakup the foxes are kept busy, and fat, with all the new arrivals migrating northward. Flocks of snow geese and sandhill cranes stop here for several weeks while waiting for the melt farther north. Ducks come singly and in pairs, some so exhausted by their flight that they fall prey to foxes. We were still setting up camp when one female pintail belly-landed in our midst, waddled a few feet to a pile of tent canvas, and slept under its shelter for two hours.

As spring progressed, each hike held the possibility of discovering a new visitor to the islands. Our own early arrival let us witness migration and add more than 40 new species to the record of birds using the islands. Among the Asiatic species we saw were bean goose, Eurasian dotterel, eye-browed thrush, white wagtail, olive tree pipit, red-throated pipit, rustic bunting, common reed bunting, brambling, slaty-backed gull and black-headed gull.

There is at least one visitor to the St. Matthew's area that foxes do not harass, the gray whale. This baleen mammoth is a long-distance traveler that fasts while in the warm waters off Baja California in winter and then swims north each summer to feed on zooplankton in the Bering Sea and Arctic Ocean.

We watched gray whales near St. Matthew's shore, often cruising closer than the walrus. In early spring we could scan the ocean and see six or more whales at one time, with a pod of Steller sea lions and perhaps a spotted seal peering at us. Bones of bowhead, humpback, blue, Baird's and killer whales have washed ashore on the islands.

When St. Matthew, Hall and Pinnacle islands are ice-bound, some seals, walrus and hardy arctic birds remain nearby if leads of open water form in the ice. A brief

Pairs of black-legged kittiwakes vie for space on the rocky ledges of St. Matthew Island.
(Kevin Schafer)

By 1982 one lone reindeer was all that was left from a herd that once numbered 6,000 before succumbing to mass starvation. Originally 29 animals were brought to St. Matthew Island in 1944 as a wartime food source for the servicemen stationed there. (Elaine Rhode)

survey in February found thick-billed murres, oldsquaws and harlequin ducks, and a small flock of pelagic cormorants. One snowy owl was seen flying over the ice near the islands.

My tiny group of biologists and those who have followed have observed the islands and their wildlife intensely in summer, but the only persons who intimately knew the islands in winter were there for a radically different reason — World War II.

War came to Alaska the summer after Pearl Harbor when Japanese troops bombed Dutch Harbor and captured the Aleutian islands of Attu and Kiska. Into this war zone where fog and gales were more hostile than the enemy, U.S. Army Intelligence sent small groups of men to strategic coasts to establish weather reporting stations and an American presence.

Ten men followed sealed orders to St. Matthew Island. On September 15, 1942, they waved goodbye to the last ship they would see for nine months. Surrounding them on the beach were mounds of supplies including parts for two Quonset huts, radio transmitters, weather instruments, food for a year, 40 tons of coal and one .30-caliber machine gun. The wind picked up to 40 mph that night, and by morning 15-foot waves were washing the coal out to sea. The men struggled all day in the chilling surf to save some of their coal.

"Gathering driftwood gave us something to do all winter," rationalized Jacob Stalker, the Alaskan Eskimo from the Noatak region assigned to the group as survival instructor.

For the next three weeks no one had to worry about keeping busy as the men raced the foul fall weather to set up camp before winter. Everything had to be hauled manually about three-quarters of a mile. "We carried it as far as our shoulders allowed," remembered John McRae, weatherman.

The last hut was completed on October 4. The next day the island was white with snow. By October 7 the signal men finally got their radio transmitter to work, and the St. Matthew weather station sent its first encoded report, one of four to be broadcast daily during the war years.

Provisions for the camp were short on flour and completely omitted salt. They had a few tins of ham, which they set aside for Thanksgiving and Christmas dinners. Stalker took charge of provisioning the camp with fresh food. He improvised a dip net and caught Dolly Varden trout from the stream and lake.

Weatherman Ben Schlegel told me: "Jake Stalker hunted ducks — eiders — and would let them hang for days before cooking them. We wouldn't let him cook the birds if they stunk too much. He also got ringed seals. We ate them, but they probably would have been better with salt."

Steller sea lions crowd Gull Rock off Pinnacle Island in the St. Matthew group. (Kevin Schafer)

Pinnacle Island, named by Capt. James Cook, looms in the Bering Sea 10 miles south of St. Matthew Island. (Kevin Schafer)

When ocean ice surrounded the island, they found tracks of polar bear. McRae remembers, "Stalker with his mukluks could stand in one with his other toe in front. We were glad the bear didn't come with the track."

They kept a fire going in the Quonsets day and night, but despite that the water in the buckets was usually frozen each morning. For recreation, the men read, listened to favorite radio programs and played pinochle. At the end of each week, they tallied pinochle scores and divided camp chores among the losers who then had to mop floors, clean huts and melt snow.

Their only brush with combat came May 1, when winter still locked the island in ice and snow. One of the men yelled, "Airplane, airplane." The radio man flashed an alert over the air and everyone rushed out to the machine gun emplacement with their 1903 Springfield rifles. Fog obscured visibility as usual for a few frantic moments, but the men finally made out the source of alarm: Two large flocks of geese flying low, offshore.

Their replacements arrived on June 25th, but the station crew didn't know that until the next day when the new lieutenant and weatherman hiked down from the north where the ship had landed.

The second weather team only used the station until late fall, when the Army consolidated quarters with a new Coast Guard camp built that summer about nine miles north on the island.

A Navy construction battalion with tractors built the

second camp. "I heard they built a 'flush toilet' camp, compared to ours," Ben Schlegel said. Indeed, there were flush toilets and running water, until winter temperatures froze the piping.

St. Matthew Island was one of the first in a series of Pacific islands to receive wartime installation of a new navigational system called Loran, still used today in a more advanced form. Electronic pulses from a master station on St. Matthew, and on Umnak Island in the Aleutians, could be intercepted by ships and aircraft and measured to calculate location.

During calm seas in September 1943, five Coast Guardsmen left the Loran station on St. Matthew in a small surfboat to follow the shore to the Army weather station to pick up a gasoline engine. Men and boat disappeared.

Station personnel were relieved yearly before ice stopped ship and amphibious plane traffic. After winter set in, aircraft would occasionally drop mail without landing. The plane making the Christmas 1944 mail drop mistakenly targeted the already abandoned Army weather station site. Severe weather and worry over safety limited the first attempt at recovery to official and first class mail. Knowledge that packages lay "so close and yet so far" teased the men all winter, but the commanding officer forbade attempting a second trip.

Another mail drop came in March but again the drop site was the same wrong location. The presence of Army codes and official documents in the mail forced an officially sanctioned trip, but bone-chilling weather delayed the men for two weeks. When the expedition finally started, it was by relay. The first team pulled a toboggan loaded with sleeping bags, guns and food for seven miles, then returned to duties at the station. The next team caught up to the toboggan and pulled it to the old weather station where they camped the night.

In the morning they started back with about 500 pounds of mail, leaving behind magazines, some Christmas packages chewed to pieces by foxes, and packages for someone not on the island. Halfway, a runner went ahead to call for the next crew which pulled the toboggan the last miles.

As the war dragged on, the military grew concerned about reaching the island regularly with supplies so in August 1944 the Coast Guard arranged capture of reindeer from the domestic herd on Nunivak Island and released them on St. Matthew.

Before a food emergency occurred, the war ended and the military abandoned the station and the island, leaving the reindeer.

From that nucleus of 24 cows and 5 bulls, the herd in 13 years grew to 1,350. By 1963, 6,000 reindeer or almost 50 per square mile grazed the island.

Their summer food of sedges, grasses and willow leaves was plentiful, and the animals responded with a high birth rate and higher body weight than other domestic reindeer.

Winter range was restricted to windswept areas blown free of snow, limiting grazing to the tundra prairies near Cape Upright and Big Lake. Here the reindeer sought lichens and willow leaves. The lichen mat was almost five inches deep when the reindeer arrived.

Jacob Stalker heard about the reindeer introduction years later while he served three terms in the new state legislature. "I tried to put through a resolution to rid the island of reindeer and put them where there was food . . . From being stationed there during the war, I knew there wasn't enough food and the winters were bad," Stalker told me.

But it was too late. By summer 1963, the winter range carried less than one-half inch of lichen. Restricted to the island, the reindeer were unable to migrate to seek new range. They had eaten themselves out of their new home in less than 20 years.

The reindeer starved to death in February and March 1964 according to Dr. David Klein of the University of Alaska, Fairbanks, who had monitored the evolution of the herd and their effect on the island's vegetation.

When Klein returned to St. Matthew in 1966, he found 42 live reindeer and no calves. The females had not given birth since the die-off.

Once there were 6,000. Then there was only one — one lone reindeer on St. Matthew in 1982 when I saw her on the tundra. How long she had been alone, I don't know; nine reindeer had been seen in 1977. She hobbled stiffly toward a knoll and bedded down with arctic foxes, voles and McKay's buntings for neighbors. A portly matron more than 20 years old, she ended an era of man's influence gone awry and was not seen again the following year.

However, other actions to alter the island were already in the works.

Under the Bering Sea more than 100 miles to the west lies an area of potential oil and gas reserves called the Navarin Basin. The oil industry saw St. Matthew as the nearest landfall and wanted to convert the southern end near Cape Upright into an offshore-drilling support base with two mile-long runways, a harbor, roads, dam and artificial lake, fuel storage tanks and quarters for 250 people.

Native corporations in Alaska proposed to accomplish this in a land trade, exchanging scattered native lands within other national wildlife refuges for a piece of St. Matthew and in turn leasing the land to oil companies.

A lawsuit was filed to block any exchange, and in November 1984 a judge ruled that the proposal was illegal and forbade any construction on St. Matthew. Since then the oil companies have used the Pribilofs as their base.

Another resource, crab, is already being harvested from nearby waters. The rocky ocean floor around St. Matthew and Hall islands is preferred habitat for blue king crab, first fished here in 1977 as an incidental catch en route to or from the red king crab fishery in Norton Sound.

In 1982 fishermen took 8.8 million pounds in three weeks; however, stocks are now drastically declining, and the 1986 season was only three days long with a quota of half a million pounds. In place of blue king crab, fishermen have recently focused on smaller opilio tanner crab in the smoother undersea plains farther west of the islands. The 1986 harvest was 35 million pounds or one-third of the total Bering Sea catch.

Our first, faraway impressions of St. Matthew and Hall islands and surrounding seas as drab, desolate and void of life were washed away, and in their place grew a respect for this marine paradise, an oceanic oasis for wildness.

A landing craft snuggles beneath the venerable *North Star III*, Bureau of Indian Affairs' supply ship which served isolated communities in western Alaska for more than 20 years.
(Penny Rennick, Staff)

Aboard the *North Star III*

For the people of Diomede, the sea has always been the route to survival. Nearby waters rich in marine life provide their sustenance. Across the sea lies the villagers' only contact with others of their culture. And things have not changed much since Western man moved into Bering Strait.

In the 20th century, residents of Ignaluk, only village on Little Diomede Island, have depended on the Bureau of Indian Affairs (BIA) for needs that could not be met by traditional subsistence activities. What could not be taken from the sea or from the skies above their tiny island was supplied by a BIA ship that called at villages along the coast of western and northern Alaska. With the arrival of the *North Star III*, heir to a long line of government resupply ships, villagers dropped whatever they were doing and headed for the beach.

Only between Diomede and the Alaskan mainland did the *North Star III* take passengers. A few years ago, I joined the *North Star III* crew in Nome for the run to Diomede. Aboard were state and federal officials completing assignments on the remote island and Diomeders returning home.

The Nome port at that time could not accommodate vessels the size of the 465-foot resupply ship which displaced more than 15,000 tons when

Whatever works. This is the easy way down for passengers going from the deck of the *North Star III* to the landing craft below. (Penny Rennick, Staff)

fully loaded. The *North Star III* anchored in the Nome roadstead, and the captain sent one of her LCMs (Landing Craft Mechanized) into the harbor to pick up waiting passengers.

The ride on the deck of the LCM across choppy Norton Sound waters was just a preliminary to the big show. As the LCM pulled alongside the *North Star III,* the larger vessel's 50-ton jumper boom swung out over the LCM, and crewmen connected the cables. The next thing the passengers knew, the entire LCM was being lifted from the sea and plunked onto the deck of the *North Star III.*

After several hours of running northwest, the *North Star III* anchored off the southwest coast of Little Diomede but well on the American side of the international boundary with the Soviet Union. Only three miles separate the two islands, and the base of Big Diomede was clearly visible under a cap of fog.

The experienced crew spread out on the deck and in the cargo holds of the *North Star III,* loading supplies onto the LCMs which then powered their way into the roaring winds of Bering Strait, and headed for Ignaluk where the villagers waited to help with the unloading. At times the winds and currents became so severe that the LCMs were in danger of being blown onto the rocks. All kinds of suggestions were offered to solve this problem, from implanting telephone poles in the sea floor to sinking an aircraft carrier. The carrier presumably would allow the tiny village to have year-round air service. But this time, strong ropes tied to a tractor on shore seemed to hold the LCM in place.

As the fuel barges and cargo barges hit the beach, brigades of villagers carried the cargo off the LCMs and onto conveyors with rollers on which boxes could be pushed up the steep, rocky hillside to the houses and store. Rocky paths made slick by a moss covering wound among the buildings. And just beyond, rocks and lush grass climbed to the horizon. Hidden in rocky crevices were thousands of crested and least auklets. Villagers were building a path to the north to an area where they picked greens for food. Another path headed over the top of the island to the other side where the Eskimos picked salmonberries.

With the cargo offloaded, the *North Star III* was ready to continue its run north along the coast. Unfortunately, weather prevented the ship from landing at Wales, so the captain chose to discharge his passengers at Brevig Mission on the south coast of the Seward Peninsula near Port Clarence.

For more than 60 years, government ships sup-plied villages along Alaska's remote coast. Their cargo has ranged from groceries, building supplies and equipment to fishing seiners, sheep and swimming pools. On southbound trips, the ship has carried tin ore from the mine at Lost River, wool from a sheep ranch in the Aleutians and meat and other reindeer products from Nunivak Island.

Beginning with the *Boxer,* a wooden sailing ship, *North Star III* was the last of a fleet of one, a unique service provided by Uncle Sam. *North Star I,* also a wooden ship, rests at Lake Union in Seattle. *North Star II* was retired to the Caribbean, where she sank. *North Star III,* originally the *Emory Victory,* and according to the *North Star* crew the only diesel-powered Victory ship ever put in operation, began her run north in 1962. She was built in 1945, and in 1949 joined the reserve fleet. In 1962 she became the *North Star III.*

Change comes even to the Bering Sea and the fall run, 1984, was the last for the *North Star III.* That tradition had come to an end. Economics and changing government philosophy led BIA to retire the vessel and contract with a private transportation company to supply the villages. The ship is on inactive reserve status and being held in Washington State's Puget Sound.

. . . Penny Rennick

The Seward Peninsula Today

Although remnants from the gold rush heyday and native traditions from even earlier times still survive on the peninsula, slow but inevitable change has taken hold. For the villagers, life is perhaps easier, but also more complicated.

Recognition of native rights brought most of the villages under the umbrella of the Alaska Native Claims Settlement Act (ANCSA), although the Siberian Yupiks of St. Lawrence chose to take control of their island and not participate in the ANCSA monetary arrangement. A judicial decision known as the "Molly Hootch" case meant new schools for most of the villages. The Bureau of Indian Affairs mandated new housing, although modern designs were perhaps more suited to the Lower 48 than to the western Alaska tundra. Washeterias and water storage tanks meant that water need no longer be hauled from hillside springs or melted from ice and snow in winter. Television, telephones, VCRs and movies are part of most village life.

City councils were organized to deal with the many branches of government and native corporations which now touch the lives of villagers. Commissions formed to handle allocation of natural resources. The Eskimo Whaling Commission allots strikes of bowhead whales in accordance with an international understanding of how much hunting pressure the bowhead population can take. The same goes for the Eskimo Walrus Commission which works with biologists to manage the harvest of Bering and Chukchi sea walrus. Without doubt, subsistence hunting and fishing still provide for the majority of Seward Peninsula residents, even those living in Nome or with close ties to Kotzebue.

With the increasing price of gold, the hulks of the floating dredges once again shake and growl, chewing up the earth as they seek the placers which have fueled so much of the peninsula's history. In summer 1987, both Dredge No. 6 near Nome's airport and Dredge No. 5 farther inland near the Icyview Subdivision of Nome were in operation. Mining engineers calculate that about 150,000 cubic yards of raw gravel scooped up by the dredges will eventually yield 3.5 tons of concentrate from which about 1,000 ounces of gold can be extracted. In

Members of the sixth-grade class at Buckland School enjoy their annual field trip to the old village site of Buckland, now called "New Site." The village site has been changed several times in the 20th century; at the time the village was located at "New Site," it was indeed a new site. Included in the class are, left to right: (back row) Evans Thomas, Tom Washington, Clara Barger, Thomas Paul Thomas, Clarence Thomas, Lori Hadley; (middle row) Perry Ballot, Peter Ballot, Phillip Geary, Johnnie Carter; (front) Bruce Ballot and Emma Hadley. (John Bania)

1986, Aspen Exploration acquired a lease on the mining claims held by Alaska Gold Co. in the Nome area. Its officials still seek the lode source for much of the gold that has come from the area's creeks, beaches and benchlands.

Offshore and a bit west of Nome, the Bima, an offshore mining vessel, dredges for placer gold in Norton Sound for Inspiration Gold Inc. At 14 stories high, size alone makes the Bima an impressive mining operation. But small-time miners, their equipment not quite so grand and sometimes slightly unorthodox, also sift the offshore gravels.

Oil companies are interested in the waters of Norton Sound also. In 1982, the Key Singapore, a jackup drilling rig, began drilling a stratigraphic test well in Norton Basin. These wells tell geologists about the subsurface geology, giving them a better idea of where to drill for oil and gas.

Tourism brings another kind of gold to the Seward

Clockwise, upper left — An Eskimo dressed in sealskins hunts the ice floes off Gambell. (Chlaus Lotscher) Crystal Milligrock and her puppy can look forward to a life of change on the Seward Peninsula where traditional ways blend with the latest trappings of contemporary American culture.
(Kory Matthews)
The Key Singapore, a jackup drilling rig, drills a Continental Offshore Stratigraphic Test (COST) well in Norton Sound 50 miles southeast of Nome. The well will help geologists determine the underlying rock layers and give them more information about the possibility of oil reservoirs.
(Courtesy of ARCO)
Dustin Gillespie (right) and his classmate Kimberly Kavairlook get a peek at Dustin's father, Don, teacher and principal at the Koyuk school. (Don Gillespie)
Libby Riddles, first woman to win the 1,049-mile Iditarod Trail Sled Dog Race, points her dog team toward Nome on the last leg of the famous crosscountry sled dog race from Anchorage to Nome.
(James Magdanz)
Dwight Milligrock of Nome proudly displays one of his excellent ivory carvings mounted on sealskin.
(Eric Luse/Alaska Division of Tourism; courtesy of Nome Convention & Visitors Bureau)

Right — The Bima, an offshore mining vessel, explores placer gold deposits offshore in Norton Sound west of Nome. Twenty-four employees are required to operate the vessel which is 525 feet high, 140 feet wide and 14 stories high. Inspiration Gold Inc. manages the vessel, which in 1987 completed its second season of dredging. Bima is named for a god of good fortune in southeast Asia. (Bruce McAllister; courtesy of Inspiration Gold Inc.) **Center** — Alaska Department of Fish and Game biologists Len Schwartz and Charlie Lean check king crab research pots in Norton Sound. (James Magdanz) **Far right** — Fog shrouds part of Lost River valley in this view looking north toward Brooks Mountain (2,898 feet), highest peak in the York Mountains. The buildings are part of a camp built in the early 1970s to mine tin. Fluorite and berrylium are also present in these mountains. (Barbara Winkley) **Lower right** — The Unalakleet River curves behind the community of Unalakleet as it flows out of the Nulato Hills on its way to Norton Sound. Portions of the river have been designated "wild and scenic" and draw an increasing number of river rafters. Fishermen also head to the Unalakleet River when the salmon runs come in each summer. (Penny Rennick, Staff)

Above — Modern transportation brings freshness and variety to Seward Peninsula stores such as the Alaska Commercial outlet at Nome. (Ernest Manewal) **Above right —** When the salmon are running, residents of Elim spend time at their fish camps near Moses Point at the mouth of the Kwiniuk River. (Trudy Genne) **Right —** Long hampered by its lack of a deep-water port and by the difficulty and expense of lightering supplies and passengers into shore, residents of Nome can finally look forward to an improved port facility. The causeway shown here is being built out to deeper water, giving ocean-going vessels a suitable place to tie up and discharge cargo. (John Harman; courtesy of Nome Convention & Visitors Bureau)

Peninsula. Most of the visitors who come on organized tours concentrate their stay in the Nome area, where they can pan for gold, ride sleds being pulled by dog teams and savor the atmosphere of a gold rush community. The conclusion of the Iditarod Trail Sled Dog Race brings visitors to the frozen Bering Sea each March.

For those with a more adventuresome bent, the outlying villages offer the best look at traditional life on the peninsula. Some, such as White Mountain, have lodges for visitors. In other villages, residents open their homes. Even a brief stop leads to thoughts of prehistoric people who followed game across the peninsula and of the Inupiats and Yupiks whose culture has evolved from these earlier people. Present-day visitors also add to the peninsula's cultural mix. Thus, as a Columbian from South America teaches a few soccer tricks to the Eskimos of Wales, he takes back with him a glimpse of Inupiat life on the last frontier.

Subsistence hunting and fishing support the 150 or so people of White Mountain, on the Fish River 15 miles northwest of Golovin. (Jim Green)

Above — A trapper's take, four red foxes hang outside a cabin at Elim. (Keith Stockard)

Above right — Computers capture the attention of students in Trudy Genne's combined third, fourth, and fifth-grade class at Elim. Intent on their computer challenge are: (first row from left) Jason Takak, Gordy Takak, Martin Murray and Rod Murray. Behind stand Nathan Nagaruk and Arnold Jemewouk. (Trudy Genne)

Right — Eric Hoberg tries his luck in the Nome River. Commercial and sport fishing underpin much of the peninsula's cash and subsistence economy. (David Roseneau)

Left — Oscar Swanson (right) and Charlie Auliye change a propane tank at Koyuk. Oscar was born in Haycock and was a student of pioneer teacher Carrie McClain. Oscar and his wife still live in Haycock, six miles from Dime Landing where his brother, Charlie, lives alone with his dog team. (Don Gillespie) **Below —** Two year-round and 30 or so summer residents share the gold rush surroundings of Candle, on the Kiwalik (Kewalik) River east of Deering. Fire about 20 years ago destroyed much of the town, but two small gold claims are still mined. (Allen Marquette)

An alert musk ox bull challenges all comers. The normal defensive behavior of these shaggy mammals is to form a circle, facing outward, with the young in the middle. This practice works fine in warding off wolves, but leaves the musk ox vulnerable to the hunter's gun. By the 19th century, musk ox had been hunted out of the Seward Peninsula. (Mark McDermott)

Goats makes themselves right at home on the farm equipment of the Green family at Pilgrim Hot Springs. For several years the Greens have used warm water from the springs to grow vegetables, continuing a tradition which began shortly after the turn of the century when miners came to the springs for a break from the rigors of sluicing gravel. The Catholic Church opened a boarding school here when the 1918 flu epidemic killed many of the peninsula's adults and left many children homeless. (Roz Goodman)

Left — Ben Pungowiyi puts the finishing touches on an intricately carved ivory tusk in the work area of his Savoonga home. (Charlie Crangle)

Above — Percy Olanna helps his mother Rita (right(and Aunt Pauline butcher a bearded seal near Brevig Mission. (James Magdanz)

Above — Ignaluk, the only village on Little Diomede Island, rises up the rocky slope on the island's west side. A little more than a mile away the International Dateline separates today from tomorrow and an international boundary separates the United States from the Soviet Union. (Stephen Bingham)

Top, right — Subsistence activities support the 150 residents of Deering on the north coast of the Seward Peninsula about 57 miles southwest of Kotzebue. (Terry Doyle)

Below, right — Subsistence and some reindeer herding provide the economic foundation for the 213 residents of Koyuk, on the north bank of Koyuk Inlet where the Koyuk River enters Norton Bay. (Bill Sheppard)

Top — Elim, population 248, rises up a slope on the northwest coast of Norton Bay, a large indentation at the northeast corner of Norton Sound. The site of an early Eskimo village, Elim grew when a reindeer reserve was set up nearby and a mission and school opened in the early 1900s. (Bill Sheppard)

Bottom — Taking its name from profitable tin deposits in the area, Tin City lies hidden near the base of Cape Mountain at the western end of the peninsula. The Air Force built a facility here about mid-century, and today Alascom employees operate a communications station. A trail over the mountain connects Tin City with the Eskimo community of Wales on Bering Strait. (Mark McDermott)

Top — A succession of lava flows beginning 65 million years ago and ending as recently as 1,000 years ago spread out across the lowlands around Imuruk Lake in Bering Land Bridge National Preserve.
(National Park Service; Bering Land Bridge National Preserve)
Bottom — The granite tors of Serpentine Hot Springs create one of the few dramatic vistas on the Seward Peninsula, an area whose scenic wonders lack the flamboyance of other parts of the state.
(Kathy O'Reilly-Doyle)

Left — The barren Mountains of the Moon rise between the Feather and Sinuk river valleys on the route between Nome and Teller. (David Roseneau)

Bottom — One of the most important archaeological sites in Seward Peninsula country, Cape Denbigh lies west of Shaktoolik at the tip of a small peninsula buttressed by the Reindeer Hills. Between 1948 and 1952, J. Louis Giddings excavated artifacts documenting a series of cultures that lived here, the oldest of which showed that people used this area when the climate was warmer than it is now. Giddings referred to these people as members of the Denbigh Flint Complex because of the skillfully flaked flint implements they left behind. (David Roseneau)

Shishmaref, population about 493, lies on Sarichef Island, one of the low-lying barrier islands along the northwestern coast of the peninsula. The town got its start as a mining supply center about the turn of the century. (Staff)

Right — The abandoned village of King Island clings to a rocky perch above the Bering Sea. Islanders gradually started leaving their homeland and moving to Nome in the 1950s for better health care, schooling and conveniences. In the 1960s the school closed and the remaining King Islanders followed their former neighbors to Nome. (Alissa Crandall)

Left — Storm clouds darken the skies above Grand Central Valley in this shot from Salmon Lake, an important landmark on the Nome-Taylor Road (commonly called the Kougarok Road). (Bruce McKenna)

Lower, left — The Kougarok Road winds 86 miles through the Sawtooth (Kigluaik) Mountains, and across the Pilgrim River valley to Taylor in the Kougarok district. As the rush to Nome attracted more miners than there was good land to stake, the hopeful gold-seekers spread out across the peninsula. Some explored the creeks of the Kougarok district, taking out enough gold to bring them back year after year. For a time, railroads carried the supplies and equipment needed to work the interior creeks. But they shut down when their profits declined, and the miners persuaded the government that a supply road was necessary to cut the prohibitive freight rates. (David Roseneau)

Bottom, right — Enterprising miners use contraptions of all kinds to separate gold from sand on the golden beaches of Nome. (Jim Simmen)

Alaska Geographic Back Issues

The North Slope, Vol. 1, No. 1. The charter issue of *ALASKA GEOGRAPHIC®. Out of print.*

One Man's Wilderness, Vol. 1, No. 2. The story of a dream shared by many, fulfilled by a few; a man goes into the Bush, builds a cabin and shares his incredible wilderness experience. Color photos. 116 pages, $9.95.

Admiralty . . . Island in Contention, Vol. 1, No. 3. An intimate and multifaceted view of Admiralty; it's geological and historical past, its present-day geography, wildlife and sparse human population. Color photos. 78 pages, $5.

Fisheries of the North Pacific: History, Species, Gear & Processes, Vol. 1, No. 4. *Out of print.* (Book edition available)

The Alaska-Yukon Wild Flowers Guide, Vol. 2, No. 1. *Out of print.* (Book edition available)

Richard Harrington's Yukon, Vol. 2, No. 2. The Canadian province with the colorful past and present. *Out of print.*

Prince William Sound, Vol. 2, No. 3. This volume explored the people and resources of the Sound. *Out of print.*

Yakutat: The Turbulent Crescent, Vol. 2, No. 4. History, geography, people — and the impact of the coming of the oil industry. *Out of print.*

Glacier Bay: Old Ice, New Land, Vol. 3, No. 1. This issue details the land and people history of southeastern Alaska's Glacier Bay National Park. *Out of print.*

The Land: Eye of the Storm, Vol. 3, No. 2. The future of one of the earth's biggest pieces of real estate. *Out of print.*

Richard Harrington's Antarctic, Vol. 3, No. 3. The Canadian photojournalist guides readers through remote and little understood regions of the Antarctic and subantarctic. More than 200 color photos and a large fold-out map. 104 pages, $8.95.

The Silver Years of the Alaska Canned Salmon Industry: An Album of Historical Photos, Vol. 3, No. 4. The grand and glorious past of the Alaska canned salmon industry. *Out of print.*

Alaska's Volcanoes: Northern Link in the Ring of Fire, Vol. 4, No. 1. Scientific overview supplemented with eyewitness accounts of Alaska's historic volcanic eruptions. *Out of print.*

The Brooks Range: Environmental Watershed, Vol. 4, No. 2. An impressive work on a truly impressive piece of Alaska — The Brooks Range. *Out of print.*

Kodiak: Island of Change, Vol. 4, No. 3. Russians, wildlife, logging and even petroleum . . . an island where change is one of the few constants. *Out of print.*

Wilderness Proposals: Which Way for Alaska's Lands? Vol. 4, No. 4. This volume presented a detailed analysis of the many Alaska lands questions. *Out of print.*

Cook Inlet Country, Vol. 5, No. 1. A visual tour of the region — its communities and its countryside. *Out of print.*

Southeast: Alaska's Panhandle, Vol. 5, No. 2. Explores southeastern Alaska's maze of fjords and islands, mossy forests and glacier-draped mountains — from Dixon Entrance to Icy Bay, including all of the state's fabled Inside Passage. Along the way are profiles of every town, together with a look at the region's history, economy, people, attractions and future. Includes large fold-out map and seven area maps. 192 pages, $12.95.

Bristol Bay Basin, Vol. 5, No. 3. Explores the land and people of the region known to many as the commercial salmon-fishing capital of Alaska. *Out of print.*

Alaska Whales and Whaling, Vol. 5, No. 4. The wonders of whales in Alaska — their life cycles, travels and travails — are examined, with an authoritative history of commercial and subsistence whaling in the North. Includes a fold-out poster of 14 major whale species in Alaska in perspective, color photos and illustrations, with historical photos and line drawings. 144 pages, $12.95.

Yukon-Kuskokwim Delta, Vol. 6, No. 1. This issue presents a close-up look at the Yupik work of the vast delta. *Out of print.*

The Aurora Borealis, Vol. 6, No. 2. The northern lights — in ancient times seen as a dreadful forecast of doom, in modern days an inspiration to countless poets. What causes the aurora, how it works, how and why scientists are studying it today and its implications for our future. 96 pages, $7.95.

Alaska's Native People, Vol. 6, No. 3. Examine the varied worlds of the Inupiat Eskimo, Yup'ik Eskimo, Athabascan, Aleut, Tlingit, Haida and Tsimshian. Included are sensitive, informative articles by Native writers, plus a large, four-color map detailing the Native villages and defining the language areas, 304 pages, $24.95.

The Stikine, Vol. 6, No. 4. River route to three Canadian gold strikes in the 1800s, the Stikine is the largest and most navigable of several rivers that flow from northwestern Canada through southeastern Alaska on their way to the sea. Illustrated with contemporary color photos and historic black-and-white; includes a large fold-out map. 96 pages, $9.95.

Alaska's Great Interior, Vol. 7, No. 1. Alaska's rich Interior country, west from the Alaska-Yukon Territory border and including the huge drainage between the Alaska Range and the Brooks Range, is covered thoroughly. Included are the region's people, communities, history, economy, wilderness areas and wildlife. Illustrated with contemporary color and black-and-white photos. Includes a large fold-out map. 128 pages, $9.95.

A Photographic Geography of Alaska, Vol. 7, No. 2. An overview of the entire state — a visual tour through the six regions of Alaska: Southeast, Southcentral/Gulf Coast, Alaska Peninsula and Aleutians, Bering Sea Coast, Arctic and Interior. Approximately 160 color and black-and-white photos and 35 maps. 192 pages, $15.95.

The Aleutians, Vol. 7, No. 3. Home of the Aleut, a tremendous wildlife spectacle, a major World War II battleground and now the heart of a thriving new commercial fishing industry. Contemporary color and black-and-white photographs, and a large fold-out map. 224 pages, $14.95.

Klondike Lost: A Decade of Photographs by Kinsey & Kinsey, Vol. 7, No. 4. An album of rare photographs and all-new text about the lost Klondike boom town of Grand Forks, second in size only to Dawson during the gold rush. $12.95.

Wrangell-Saint Elias, Vol. 8, No. 1. Mountains, including the continent's second- and fourth-highest peaks, dominate this international wilderness that sweeps from the Wrangell Mountains in Alaska to the southern Saint Elias range in Canada. Includes a large fold-out map. 144 pages, $9.95.

Alaska Mammals, Vol. 8, No. 2. From tiny ground squirrels to the powerful polar bear, and from the tundra to the magnificent whales inhabiting Alaska's waters, this volume includes 80 species of mammals found in Alaska. 184 pages, $12.95.

The Kotzebue Basin, Vol. 8, No. 3. Examines northwestern Alaska's thriving trading area of Kotzebue Sound and the Kobuk and Noatak river basins, lifelines of the region's Inupiat Eskimos, early explorers, and present-day, hardy residents. 184 pages, $12.95.

Alaska National Interest Lands, Vol. 8, No. 4. Following passage of the bill formalizing Alaska's national interest land selections (d-2 lands), longtime Alaskans Celia Hunter and Ginny Wood review each selection, outlining location, size, access, and briefly describing the region's special attractions. 242 pages, $14.95.

Alaska's Glaciers, Vol. 9, No. 1. Examines in depth the massive rivers of ice, their composition, exploration, present-day distribution and scientific significance. 144 pages, $10.95.

Sitka and Its Ocean/Island World, Vol. 9, No. 2. From the elegant capital of Russian America to a beautiful but modern port, Sitka, on Baranof Island, has become a commercial and cultural center for southeastern Alaska. 128 pages, $9.95.

Islands of the Seals: The Pribilofs, Vol. 9, No. 3. Great herds of northern fur seals drew Russians and Aleuts to these remote Bering Sea islands where they founded permanent communities and established a unique international commerce. 128 pages, $9.95.

Alaska's Oil/Gas & Minerals Industry, Vol. 9, No. 4. Experts detail the geological processes and resulting mineral and fossil fuel resources that are now in the forefront of Alaska's economy. Illustrated with historical black-and-white and contemporary color photographs. 216 pages, $12.95.

Adventure Roads North: The Story of the Alaska Highway and Other Roads in *The MILEPOST®*, Vol. 10, No. 1. From Alaska's first highway — the Richardson — to the famous Alaska Highway, first overland route to the 49th state, text and photos provide a history of Alaska's roads and take a mile-by-mile look at the country they cross. 224 pages, $14.95.

ANCHORAGE and the Cook Inlet Basin, Vol. 10, No. 2. "Anchorage country" . . . the Kenai, the Susitna Valley, and Matanuska. Heavily illustrated in color and including three illustrated maps . . . one an uproarious artist's forecast of "Anchorage 2035." 168 pages, $14.95.

Alaska's Salmon Fisheries, Vol. 10, No. 3. The work of *ALASKA®* magazine Outdoors Editor Jim Rearden, this issue takes a comprehensive look at Alaska's most valuable commercial fishery. 128 pages, $12.95.

Up the Koyukuk, Vol. 10, No. 4. Highlights the Koyukuk region of north-central Alaska . . . the wildlife, fauna, Native culture and more. 152 pages, $14.95.

Nome: City of the Golden Beaches, Vol. 11, No. 1. The colorful history of Alaska's most famous gold rush town has never been told like this before. Illustrated with hundreds of rare black-and-white photos, the book traces the story of Nome from the crazy days of the 1900 gold rush. 184 pages, $14.95.

Alaska's Farms and Gardens, Vol. 11, No. 2. An overview of the past, present, and future of agriculture in Alaska, and a wealth of information on how to grow your own fruit and vegetables in the north. 144 pages, $12.95.

Chilkat River Valley, Vol. 11, No. 3. This issue explores the mountain-rimmed valley at the head of the Inside Passage, its natural resources, and those hardy residents who make their home along the Chilkat. 112 pages, $12.95.

Alaska Steam, Vol. 11, No. 4. A pictorial history of the Alaska Steamship Company pioneering the northern travel lanes. Compiled by Lucile McDonald. More than 100 black-and-white historical photos. 160 pages. $12.95.

Northwest Territories, Vol. 12, No. 1. An in-depth look at some of the most beautiful and isolated land in North America. Compiled by Richard Harrington. 148 color photos. 136 pages. $12.95.

Alaska's Forest Resources, Vol. 12, No. 2 examines the majestic and valuable forests of Alaska. Nearly 200 historical black-and-white and color photos. 200 pages. $14.95.

Alaska Native Arts and Crafts, Vol. 12, No. 3. An in-depth look at the art and artifacts of Alaska's Native people. More than 200 full color photos. 215 pages. $17.95.

Our Arctic Year, Vol. 12, No. 4. Vivian and Gil Staender's simple, compelling story of a year in the wilds of the Brooks Range of Alaska, with only birds, nature and an unspoiled land. They share their discoveries, and their reactions to a year of isolation with time to sense their surroundings. Over 100 color photos. 150 pages. $12.95.

Where Mountains Meet the Sea: Alaska's Gulf Coast, Vol. 13, No. 1. Alaskan's first-hand descriptions of the 850-mile arc that crowns the Pacific Ocean from Kodiak and surrounding islands to Cape Yakataga. Included is a historical overview of this area, and a close look at the geological forces that constantly reshape its landscape. More than 300 photos. 191 pages. $14.95.

Backcountry Alaska, Vol. 13, No. 2. Alaska Geographic Society tabletop version of *The Alaska Wilderness Milepost™* — "Where the Roads End . . . the Real Alaska Begins." A full-color look at the remote communities and villages of Alaska. How to get there, what to do and where to stay. 224 pages, $14.95.

British Columbia Coast/The Canadian Inside Passage, Vol. 13, No. 3. Where to go, how to get there, what you'll find on the B.C. Coast west of the Coast Mountain divide, including Vancouver Island and the Queen Charlottes. Brief historical background (indigenous residents, fur trade, exploration, European settlers) and current conditions. Includes large fold-out map. $14.95.

Lake Clark/Lake Iliamna Country, Vol. 13, No. 4. This issue chronicles the human and natural history of the region that many claim has a sampling of all the best that Alaska has to offer in natural beauty. 152 pages, $14.95.

Dogs of the North, Vol. 14, No. 1. The first men to cross the Bering Land Bridge probably brought dogs to Alaska. Just when man brought dog and sled together is unknown, but they were indispensable to the Eskimo long before white men arrived, and as indispensable to the newcomers in both civilian and military pursuits. Decades before machines took over winter transport, racing introduced sled-dogs to a new and more glamorous roll. This issue examines the development of northern breeds from the powerful husky and malemute to the fearless little Tahltan bear dog, the evolution of the dog sled, uses of dogs, and the history of sled-dog racing from the All-Alaska Sweepstakes of 1908 to the nationally televised Iditarod of today. Lavishly illustrated, 120 pages, $14.95.

South/Southeast Alaska, Vol. 14, No. 2. The final chain in the **ALASKA GEOGRAPHIC®** issues covering the famous Inside Passage, this one provides an intimate view of the lands and waterways from Dixon Entrance to Sumner Strait, from the crest of the Coast Range to the open ocean. Here, where nature is lavish with renewable resources, human history began with the robust Tlingits, its second chapter is still in progress, and its potential is seemingly without limit. 120 pages, heavily illustrated, detailed pull-out map. U.S., $14.95; Canada, $18.95.

COMING ATTRACTION:
The Upper Yukon Basin, Vol. 14, No. 4, 1987. Headwaters for one of the continent's mightiest rivers and gateway for some of Alaska's earliest pioneers, the Upper Yukon Basin lies nestled between the mountains along the Yukon Territory-Northwest Territories border and the giants of the coastal Saint Elias Range. Yukoner Monty Alford describes this remote corner of the continent where the fur trade, mining and tourism have provided a livelihood for the less than 30,000 hardy settlers. Illustrated with contemporary color and historical black-and-white photographs. Available late fall, 1987.

ALL PRICES SUBJECT TO CHANGE.

Your $30 membership in the Alaska Geographic Society includes 4 subsequent issues of *ALASKA GEOGRAPHIC®*, the Society's official quarterly. Please add $4 for non-U.S. membership.

Additional membership information available upon request. Single copies of the *ALASKA GEOGRAPHIC®* back issues are also available. When ordering, please make payments in U.S. funds and add $1 postage/handling per copy. To order back issues send your check or money order and volumes desired to:

The Alaska Geographic Society

P.O. Box 93370, Anchorage, Alaska 99509